THE POST-PANDEMIC
LIBERAL ARTS COLLEGE

A MANIFESTO
FOR REINVENTION

STEVEN VOLK & BETH BENEDIX

The Post-Pandemic Liberal Arts College: A Manifesto for Reinvention

Steven Volk
Beth Benedix

Belt Publishing

Printed in the United States of America

First edition 2020

1 2 3 4 5 6 7 8 9

ISBN: 978-1-948742-84-9

Belt Publishing
3143 W. 33rd Street, Cleveland, Ohio 44109
www.beltpublishing.com

Book design by Meredith Pangrace & David Wilson
Cover design by David Wilson

Dedication

Steve

To Dinah, Jonah, and Anna

Beth

This book is dedicated, with gratitude, to
my students. What a privilege it has been
to learn with and from you.

"Historically, pandemics have forced humans to break with the past and imagine their world anew. This one is no different. It is a portal, a gateway between one world and the next. We can choose to walk through it, dragging the carcasses of our prejudice and hatred, our avarice, our data banks and dead ideas, our dead rivers and smoky skies behind us. Or we can walk through lightly, with little luggage, ready to imagine another world. And ready to fight for it."

—*Arundhati Roy*

"In this new environment, higher-ed institutions that are less in love with tradition and more in love with their students will be the ones that thrive."

—*Michael Sorrell, president of Paul Quinn College*

INTRODUCTION

Warren Buffett once remarked, "You only find out who is swimming naked when the tide goes out." Within the world of colleges and universities, the COVID-19 pandemic of 2020 sucked the tide out in a heartbeat, revealing many of the fractures that had already been pulling higher education apart. The financial breaches are most readily visible—all but a top tier of wealthy institutions are teetering on the edge of disaster, caught between rising costs and declining public support. And for small liberal arts colleges (SLACs), reliant as they are on a residential model, the shutdown and its economic fallout have had particularly dire financial implications.

But we believe that this crisis involves a lot more than financial instability. This crisis is existential and moral in nature. The financial straits many SLACs find themselves in serve as a vivid marker of the ways they have failed to deliver on many of their core promises. At the risk of sounding like Cassandras, we believe the pandemic is issuing a stark ultimatum to these institutions of higher education: change or die. The question is, of course, why should anyone care? Liberal arts colleges are a particularly American innovation. They primarily serve undergraduates who opt for breadth and depth in the arts and sciences, rather than pursuing a narrower vocational, technical, or preprofessional approach employed by other institutions of higher education. They are usually small in size, residential, and they thrive on "high-touch," "face-to-face" teaching methods. There are not many of them. In 2018, fewer than 200 four-year colleges and universities (out of more than 4,000 across the United States) focused on arts and sciences undergraduate education (Carnegie Classification). Graduates from SLACs account for less than 1 percent of all college graduates every year. Their critics, and there are many of them, charge that liberal arts colleges don't prepare their graduates for the labor market, they are absurdly expensive, and they coddle their students to boot! The only stories about them that make the news seem to be ones that feature students shouting down unwanted speakers, harassing local merchants, or refusing to read novels that "offend" them. So for many families who are struggling to pay the rent, and who are now staring into an historically deep economic abyss, the survival of residential liberal arts colleges is just not on their radar. Nature, as Alfred Lord Tennyson reminds us, is "red in tooth and claw." Let nature take its course, the thinking goes, and just let the SLACs shut down.

We, Steve and Beth, shudder at the thought. We don't want SLACs to die. We love the two institutions where we have taught (collectively) for over half a century, the extraordinary students who have shaped our lives, and the rich, vibrant, multifaceted approach to meaning-making that marks the liberal arts tradition. And we're not alone in our high regard for these institutions. Study after study has confirmed the transformative power of a liberal arts education, finding that SLACs "produce a pattern of consistently positive student outcomes not found in any other type of American higher education institution." (Oakley 7, Kuh 122). But SLACs have to change if they are going to remain true to their historical missions while also being attentive to the challenges of the contemporary moment. Liberal arts colleges are, by definition, small. If you were to stretch Union College in Schenectady, New York, to be the size of the University of Michigan, you no longer would have a liberal arts college. And that size dictates selectivity. Yet our central argument in this book is that instead of using their small size to become more integrated, inclusive, collaborative, and visionary, SLACs have instead transformed into privileged and exclusionary spaces. To a troubling degree, they have allowed their selectivity to act as a restrictive barrier, narrowing and homogenizing those who can access this kind of education. The colleges we are so passionate to protect have been building walls around themselves that make it harder for people who truly want this kind of an education to get it. Low-income students are pushed away by the high price of a liberal arts education and are thwarted by an unjust, discriminatory K–12 educational system that makes it clear they shouldn't even bother applying. Black and Brown students are discouraged by the knowledge that they will not find many peers, faculty, or staff who look like them at SLACs, and they're disheartened by the realization that if they *do* get in, they will be required to check their cultures at the door and assimilate into an historically white environment. And for those students who do make it over the walls, who weather an insanely competitive admission system that forces them to take every AP class under the sun, win their state's science competition, invent a cure for Alzheimer's, and write an admissions essay expressing both their uniqueness *and* the ways in which they have done exactly the same things as every other applicant? Those students arrive to campus anxious and exhausted rather than

11

energized and ready to think on their own terms.

This book calls for these walls to be torn down. We want small liberal arts colleges to reimagine themselves as part of a new and expansive culture, to rededicate themselves as spaces that will serve, educate, and learn from those who desperately want to attend them. This renewed focus, we argue, is the best path forward for the survival of these colleges. It is the best way to address the concerns of people, including parents and prospective students, who have been dismayed by rising costs and who have grown distrustful of schools' stated goals.

We feel the urgency of this work more now than ever before. Everything about the COVID-19 crisis has underscored the importance of expanding the model of liberal education, which stresses studying broadly across disciplines as well as deeply within a few, encourages collaboration and compassion, and couples risk-taking with responsibility. We are living through a crisis that has made a mockery of rigidly segmented approaches to problem solving or educational models that train students for jobs that robots might take over tomorrow. Controlling this pandemic will require not just the specialized knowledge of virologists and epidemiologists, but the combined efforts of health care providers, doctors and nurses, urban planners and engineers, economists, logistics experts, journalists, public officials, and many others. And they are all going to have to collaborate in teams, understanding where their specialties merge into the expertise of others. The shutdown has also taught us more broadly about what we need to survive. In a new era of social distancing, we have quickly come to appreciate the companionship and good cheer that writers, artists, musicians, and filmmakers bring us. In a time marked by fear and anxiety, we have come to more readily understand the moral suasion of empathy. In a world of intensifying nationalism, we observe that viruses ignore borders and that we will only be able to solve wicked problems like pandemics or climate change through global cooperation. In short, this crisis has shown us the importance of the exact kinds of knowledge, skills, and dispositions that are the beating heart of small liberal arts colleges.

On May 25, 2020, as we were in the midst of writing this book, Minneapolis police officer Derek Chauvin knelt on George Floyd's neck for eight minutes and forty-six seconds, killing him in broad daylight as three additional officers, ignoring the pleas of a crowd who had gathered around to bear witness, did nothing to stop him. This was just the latest of so many grotesquely violent killings of Black men, women, and children by police officers. As we watched, a country already reeling from a pandemic exploded in furious protest, and it struck us with renewed urgency that our colleges also must do much more to address the historical legacy of anti-Black racism. Despite the missions that many liberal arts colleges espouse—to promote social justice, equity, and access; to build welcoming, diverse, inclusive learning communities; and to enact what the schools value, not what the corporate marketplace dictates—we find that SLACs are actually reinforcing the insidious patterns that manifest most graphically in anti-Black violence and that have been revealed (yet again) by the unequal toll the novel coronavirus is extracting from Black and Brown bodies. *This* crisis forces us to look at who *we*—liberal arts colleges—have become, at the fact that many elite colleges admit more students from the top 1 percent of income earners than the bottom 60 percent, and that students, faculty, and administrators of color are significantly and historically underrepresented at our institutions.

We're struck by the paradox in all of this. The system that we willingly replicate has placed us as gatekeepers, but has also stripped us of our power to be who we say we want to be. It seems to us that we have collectively handed over our power to forces that none of us really support. If SLACs want to emerge whole on the other side of this pandemic, if they want to truly embrace their missions and be who they say they want to be, they must reclaim that power. SLACs have to imagine and enact a new set of practices and structures—a new culture—that removes them from the toxic culture in which they currently find themselves and that challenges the injustices embedded in these institutions. This is a moral imperative as much as it is a financial one.

We write this book—to borrow Kevin Gannon's phrase (and the spirit of that phrase)—out of a "radical hope" that we *can* change our institutions, that we *can* create a wholly new paradigm that will harness the promise of SLACs to be authentic engines of equality, shattering the "crisis of cowardice" that has kept many of our institutions immobilized for too long (Ellis). The statements circulated by many liberal arts college presidents in the days following George Floyd's murder are one indication that our hope may not be misplaced. These statements have been forceful in their description of the anguish that results from still finding ourselves immersed in a world that views African Americans as less than human and unworthy of dignity. These statements are also determined in their call for liberal arts colleges to dedicate themselves to fighting for justice (Val Smith, Swarthmore), and to "work so that the marginalized are no longer at the edges but rather at the center" (Carmen Twillie Ambar, Oberlin). It is, it must be, the work of our institutions to take responsibility, support risk, and change the system we inhabit. The structure of this book is built on a simple assumption. In order to shape the future, we have to be able to identify and name those conditions that restrain us in the present. SLACs have to acknowledge unflinchingly who they are before they can become who they most want to be. Part 1 is intended as a snapshot of the days leading up to, and the weeks following, the pandemic shutdown, the moment in the spring of 2020 when campuses came "screeching to a halt." Focusing in particular on Beth's experience with DePauw's closure, the section points to the ways the abrupt transition to virtual learning demonstrated how vital the residential component is to the educational mission of SLACs and the ways that this residential culture is currently falling short of achieving its full potential. Part 2 lays out some of the broad economic and ideological forces (neoliberalism and structural racism) that have undermined higher education in general, and then examines the specific forces that have pressured small liberal arts colleges away from their proclaimed missions. Finally, part 3 offers our vision for reinvention, our "manifesto." It charts the key changes we believe SLACs can and must make to address their structural inequities and to create a more dynamic, equitable, and relevant classroom culture. Though we are decidedly not economists, we suggest ways to reconcile one of the most intractable problems facing SLACs: how they can square their economic constraints with the moral imperatives embedded in their diverse yet kindred mission statements. Liberal arts colleges must be financially sustainable if they are to have a future, but they also must admit students *without regard to financial need* if they are to be true to their stated missions of equity and social justice. To argue for anything less is to maintain that the institutions are more valuable than the principles which define them.

A note on who tells "our" story in this book. As you'll see, the two of us often use the first-person voice to talk about many of the problems and challenges facing small liberal arts colleges. "We"—that is, Steve and Beth—often refer to "our" colleges, "our" missions," and what "we" have to do to change SLACs. Because we both have spent our careers teaching at small liberal arts colleges, it shouldn't be surprising that we view many issues from a faculty perspective. But over the decades we have learned invaluable lessons from students, staff, administrators, and community members. On a broader level, then, the "we" that populates this book includes everyone who has a stake in the survival and success of SLACs. Besides faculty, administrators, professional staff, and students, the "we" includes dining hall workers, admissions counselors, coaches, residence hall directors, service workers, lab technicians, prospective students, trustees, parents, alumni, and many more. The "we" imagined here is expansive rather than exclusionary, it is a way for us to frame and talk about the communal effort that's required for this process of profound reimagining we're recommending.

What is at stake in this discussion are SLACs' very reasons for being. It is our hope that liberal arts colleges will seize the opportunities opened by the dual challenges of the pandemic and the virulent persistence of anti-Black racism to reclaim the power that they have ceded to neoliberal pressures, the siren call of presumed meritocracy, the ranking agencies, and our own tradition-bound practices, and use it instead to make colleges that are affordable, inclusive, and transformative. We invite you to take this leap of faith with us.

PART ONE

SCREECHING
TO A HALT

PRELUDE

On March 11, 2020, at 8:12 p.m., as the State of Indiana began to perceive the magnitude of COVID-19, the members of the DePauw University community (like so many others) received an email announcing the suspension of in-class instruction. Over the next four days, the deadline for students to leave campus—with all of their belongings—was pushed forward several times, eventually landing on March 16, at 5:00 p.m. At that point, any student who had not been granted eligibility to remain on campus (235 students) had to be gone. As the news settled in, students scrambled to spend time with one another. Pop-up ensembles claimed the halls of the performing arts center. The local inn faced such a swarm of students that the owners stopped serving alcohol. Seniors were hit full in the face with the realization that their college experience, as they had known it up to this point, had just ended. All of those memory-making, pregraduation rituals they'd been dreaming about since freshman year were now gone.

Seven and a half hours before the email came, I (Beth) was teaching *Waiting for Godot* in my existential literature course.

Wanting to breathe new energy into the class and give us a chance to inhabit and perform scenes from the play, we had relocated for the week to an auditorium in the oldest building on campus. The auditorium, which had formerly served as a chapel, had vaulted ceilings arching over wooden pews and a defunct pipe organ that was lofted in the corner. Now it housed more mundane events—lectures, the occasional faculty meeting, student recitals—and the walls were hung with portraits of DePauw's presidents and (in a less-than-subtle jab at the patriarchal legacy of the place) a relatively recent series of portrait-sized photos by a faculty artist that represented women from various contingents of the DePauw community (though there were no students). Most of the class sat sprawled in a circle on the stage. The high-backed leather chairs reserved for esteemed visitors had been pushed aside. A handful of students, a buzzing lethargy in their collective and individual poses, had claimed seats in the window sills or on the stairs leading up to the stage.

The irony that we were slated that day to process Beckett's absurdist classic was deafening: students had been alerted earlier that this email was coming, and that they would know by 3:00 p.m. whether or not face-to-face classes were going to be cancelled for the remainder of the semester. Now we were, literally, just waiting. In another class I had taught earlier that day, there was no less irony: that morning we were making our way through *The Trial*. None of us could escape the fact that the concept of "indefinite postponement," one of three possible outcomes for the accused Joseph K., had just taken on real-life contours that were too surreal, even for Kafka. What else was there to talk about other than the ways the college's imminent announcement stood to change everyone's reality? Time was already carved into a "before" and "after," though none of us knew what that "after" would look like.

The next few days were a blur. Some faculty cancelled

the remaining two days of classes. Some doubled down on expectations, insisting scheduled exams be taken on those days rather than postponed until a less anxious time. Some just tried to stay the course, using the final two days as an opportunity to bring some semblance of closure to the chapter of in-person learning that, until that moment, we had all taken for granted. "Business as usual" vied with "panic" as the plan for the rest of the semester started to take shape. Faculty, the vast majority of whom had no experience whatsoever with "virtual," "remote," or "distance" learning, were being asked to quickly adapt their classes to an online platform, playing out in microcosm the same scenario that had become the subject of countless articles, chat rooms, special issues of academic journals, Facebook groups, and blogs. Those discussions— about contingency plan learning, makeshift learning, making-the-best-of-it-learning—grew no less virulently than the virus itself. It was "panic-gogy," as Sean Michael Morris, director of the Digital Pedagogy Lab and senior instructor in Education and Human Development at the University of Colorado, Boulder, put it.

Toward the end of the last day of face-to-face classes at DePauw, a senior music student, who was working with me on their (this student's preferred pronoun) honors thesis, came to my office, pulling with them a nearly empty suitcase that had been filled with their extraordinary signature handmade hats. They'd been giving the hats out to lucky recipients all day, a much-needed gesture of whimsy. They described the unexpected sweetness and vulnerability of the liminal space in which we'd all found ourselves. How suddenly it seemed we now stopped and listened when we asked others, "How are you?" How the myriad impromptu jam sessions that students formed reminded them of what they were most passionate about—being and playing and creating together. In this liminal space, this student told me, "we rediscovered our priorities ... and going to class wasn't one of them."

"I'm just afraid it will all go back to the way it was before," they said, "the way we're spending time together now is so much more authentic, so much more real."

There was also a palpable antagonism in the air. That antagonism had generally been latent in the structure of top-down classroom dynamics, but now it was magnified and laid bare by the stress the structure was under. This dynamic led to a kind of standoff. The perceived defiance of these shifting (or crystallizing) student priorities was met by the draconian measures of some faculty members, an insistence that the students' priorities should remain centered on the classroom, and in some cases, on course material entirely disconnected from the frightening and ever-shifting reality that was changing by the hour. Students described a refrain that they kept hearing in the plans that were evolving for their "online" learning: a need to devise strategies that would keep them from cheating. The default assumption from faculty seemed to be that students would resort to academic dishonesty. It was a stark either-or assumption writ large: *either* we (the faculty) keep them (the students) in line and focused on the task at hand, *or* everything will fall apart and the course material will go unlearned.

We include these idiosyncratic details to suggest that, in the small liberal arts colleges that the two of us call home, everything was already in the mix even before the semester was brought to a screeching halt by the coronavirus pandemic. The vestiges of tradition stubbornly asserted themselves on that chapel wall, in the pushback against that stubborn tradition in the form of the newer portraits, in the absence of student faces from the portrait collection of institutional representatives, in the expectations that students would cheat, in the students' explicit naming of the fact that classes weren't a priority, and in the profound ambivalence that something sweet and beautiful could happen even in the midst of the antagonism that always, always seemed to be humming in the background. Rebecca Barrett Fox's blog post, "Please do a bad job of putting your courses online," is a time-capsule-worthy artifact in this regard. Her post, and its intentionally provocative title (one angry reader called it "clickbait"), set off a slew of responses. The majority of readers found her advice to be a relief, practical and compassionate, but a vocal minority was clearly incensed by her charge to lower expectations and resist change. The post's comment section is, unfortunately, a study in the lack of civility, full of accusatory, demeaning inflections and the zero-sum language and either-or thinking that too often mark the way faculty members talk to one another and to students, pandemic or not. It also points to how empty the term "student-centered" has become. Virtually every comment includes some version of the term, but these versions are often radically at odds with one another. This is a perfect example of the way that even though higher education may have come screeching to a halt, the nature of the conversations we were having in this "halted" moment mimicked the ones we had been having all along. And, along with the student of the extraordinary hats, both Steve and I share the fear that everything will go back to "the way it was before" once this is all over. This is not a place we want to go back to.

Adventures in Virtual Learning

The series of emails leading up to the closure of DePauw's campus tell a story of tempered caution, a warding off of the seemingly not-terribly-present-danger of being blindsided by a pandemic. On January 24, the college's office of communications sent a message to the entire community on "coronavirus awareness and prevention," providing "key resources" and CDC recommendations (primarily with regard to "avoiding non-essential travel to Wuhan, China"). On March 2, there was a follow-up message, an update to CDC guidelines on prevention and travel, along with a message of calming assurance: "while the risk of coronavirus COVID-19 in the U.S. remains low at this time and there are no confirmed cases in Indiana or at DePauw University, we continue to prepare for a potential outbreak or pandemic." Less than a week before the notification of the closing of campus, on March 7, faculty received an email from the vice president of academic affairs. The college was, as the email stated:

> taking the cautionary and preparatory step of suspending in-person class instruction during the two days leading up to spring break (Thursday 3/19/20 and Friday 3/20/20). This suspension will provide faculty with the opportunity to develop, revise and/or test plans for online instruction should that be needed due to a future suspension of in-person class meetings (e.g., as a result of COVID-19 cases on campus, weather emergencies, etc.) or because some students cannot attend classes in-person due to illness.

Despite the tempered caution, and despite the best efforts of those tasked with devising preparations and a plan, we *were* blindsided. Four days before the unprecedented event of closing a residential campus for the duration of the semester and without an end in sight, the language was still entirely hypothetical, the pandemic just one emergency scenario among any number of hypothetical others. All of a sudden, we were unmoored. A week of incredulousness, denial, anger, fear—accelerated stages of mourning—slid into another, a week that had been originally scheduled to be our spring break. And then that week slid into a full-on plunge into a brave new world of teaching and learning that none of us had any clue how to navigate.

As the adventure took hold, my students (with whom I was "meeting" in independent and small group sessions on Google Hangout—students chose which model they preferred) described their new realities and what it felt like to have entered into this strange learning space that none of us were prepared for. In the first week, the stress on some of their faces was hard to miss. One student in particular looked lost and drained; ten minutes into our conversation, she covered her face in her hands, tucked her legs underneath her with a jolting motion on the bed she was sitting on, and let out a despondent sigh. "I just wish this would all be over," she said. Most students reported feeling bored, completely unable to focus, anxious, and sad.

The range of learning experiences varied widely from class to class. Some faculty members entirely missed the action, some created asynchronous video content that students could watch on their own, and others conducted synchronous Zoom meetings for twenty or more students that lasted an hour or more. Students reported various levels of success with these meetings. In some cases, the technology held up well and they were glad for the chance to see others and to think about something other than COVID-19. In others, the platform couldn't sustain the traffic, people talked over each other without being able to hear what others were saying, or the professor lectured in real time to students who, zoning out, used the time to work on other projects. Some faculty, undeterred by the curveball the pandemic had thrown, continued to deliver their course content without any attempts to pare it down or make it relevant to the current situation. Others entirely revamped their classes to accommodate the new reality. In most cases that students described, this revamping meant an easing up on requirements that could no longer be fulfilled in this new setting. Some students, however, suggested that their professors were upping the ante, adding considerably more assignments than they had included in the course's original iteration, assignments that felt to them like busywork or box-checking, designed primarily for the purpose of taking attendance rather than as a vehicle for learning the material.

A month into the online transition, a DePauw senior sent the following email to the vice president of academic affairs (VPAA) with the subject heading, "This isn't working" (the following is excerpted and included with the student's permission):

> I really struggle to write this email. I had a horribly lonely freshman year here at DePauw. … I contemplated transferring every day. … Two things kept me at DePauw: First, I applied for and was offered a position [as an RA] for sophomore year. This effectively put me into a large caring community. … Secondly, I had great reverence for DePauw's academics and embraced the liberal arts philosophy. Academics were challenging and from time to time I would resent certain assignments or readings … but I did get so much enjoyment from the product and from the work. Unfortunately, that is no longer the case.
>
> I know the circumstances of this pandemic and the extended, mandated period of social distancing is new for all of us. I know it was impossible to plan for and has been exceptionally difficult to reorient curriculum to work for the circumstances. While my current professors have been very accommodating

and understanding, the plain fact is that reorienting the curriculum has been a disaster for me and every single peer I've communicated with. I can tell that the reorientation has had major consequences on faculty—some have admitted it—and I can only imagine the difficult decisions that administration is having to make throughout this precarious crisis.

I say all this to show that the expansive repercussions of COVID-19 are not lost on me—I'm not sending you this email because I'm having a hard time and I want some help; I'm sending this email because this isn't working. This isn't working for anybody. ...

I've been ripped away from my home of the last four years. That was, obviously, the right call; however, I did almost everything for four years inside a one square mile plot of land. I lived, worked, slept, ate, felt every range of emotion, calibrated every facet of my academic life within that one square mile. All of my routine, all of my community which I rely on to stabilize me and help me be successful at DePauw is unavoidably gone. Seniors, like myself, have the added burden of never being able to regain that particular stability or get any semblance of closure for having lost it. One of DePauw's defining characteristics is its status as a residential campus. The purpose of this residentiality, as stated on the DePauw website, is that "by living on campus, DePauw students engage in diverse communities that foster learning with & from others." I've grown accustomed to this system, and it has completely fallen away, leaving me floundering.

I would be remiss not to address my privilege. My home life is stable, my parents have kept their jobs and aren't currently worried about losing them, my family has remained healthy, systems in general are very much stacked in my favor, and yet the work I'm supposed to do feels impossible—the task seemingly insurmountable.

I wish I could offer a perfect solution—if there was one I'm sure I wouldn't be feeling the way that I am. I don't want to make a drastic recommendation that won't be taken seriously, though I have some of those recommendations. I don't want to make a milquetoast recommendation that won't end up making me feel better. I don't want you to not take this seriously because I don't offer a solution. All I know for sure is that I can't keep feeling like this, and that my peers can't keep feeling like this, and that my professors can't keep feeling like this. None of us deserve to be feeling like this, and this feeling is not simply an unavoidable consequence of the pandemic. The current demands on all of us, while designed to be less than usual, are breaking me.

Faculty and administration have been vocally understanding, but it really doesn't seem like you all understand. Again, I know this is equally as hard on you all, that's why I write this email. This really isn't working.

The rawness is striking, especially the capacity this student has to parse out his feelings of frustration from his sense of empathy. Even more striking is his assumption that the

VPAA would lend a compassionate ear. From the outside, this assumption might look like entitlement, even as this student calls himself out for his privilege. It might look like melodrama, a catalog of relatively small losses to experience in the grand scheme of such a mammoth, global disruption. But what strikes us—from the inside—is the weight this student places on the community that he was forced to leave behind, and his contention that the loss of that community is at the center of his feelings of futility, paralysis, and inertia, feelings he suspects others share. What strikes us is his assurance that his assumption about the VPAA was anything but misplaced, but rather an intuitive guess that this figure who was in charge would respond in a manner consistent with the thoughtful, genuine, self-aware, and compassionate approach that had marked the student's other interactions on campus.

The VPAA did. He thanked the student and went on to explicitly match the student's "transparency" (as he describes it) with his own. He candidly expressed the admiration he felt for this student, his care for the student's anxiety concerning his own experience and that of his peers, his sadness that this unprecedented moment has caused such disruption and pain for the student body, and his agreement with the contention that there were no good solutions to the situation in which DePauw found itself. He exhibited great humility in not having answers, and he provided the student with resources for self-care that he acknowledged "might not be helpful."

There's one line in the student's email that we keep coming back to in the midst of it all, however: "this feeling is not simply an unavoidable consequence of the pandemic." We zero in on the double negative—"not unavoidable"—a suggestion that there's nothing necessary or given or inevitable about the toll the shutdown has taken on all of us. It could have gone another way, any number of other ways. For some of our students, it *has* gone another way. For some of our students, the shutdown has served as a source of relief and liberation, an escape from an increasingly exhausting and soul-sucking grind. For some, who struggle with social anxiety or depression, who are tired of a lusterless classroom dynamic, who question the worth of the education they're paying so much for, the shutdown has provided a chance to finally pursue their learning on their own terms. And so we tend to read into this double negative something else: however aberrant and unprecedented the catalyst for this screeching halt may be, it was inevitable. It was just a matter of time.

The Hypocrisy-Cynicism Complex

Two weeks before DePauw's campus closed, the student of the extraordinary hats came to talk with me about their thesis. The premise of the thesis now seems altogether prophetic, shedding light on our shared sense that SLACs have been plummeting headlong toward a point of no return. Steve and I thought it deserved some attention in this discussion.

Inspired by the complicated nuances of the relationship between Nietzsche and Wagner, this student conjured up a fictional world in which to play: a small liberal arts college of the future that is debilitated by nihilism. The dean (worried mainly about dropping enrollments and the hit the endowment is taking) enlists a philosophy professor, Walter Picardy, to pull the student body out of the dumps and help them envision another perspective. Through the medium of a radio broadcast, Picardy calls on his love of Nietzsche to rally the students (and himself), but in the process, he becomes more and more unsure of the way out. Hilarity ensues (sort of), but also dread. The cast of characters featured in the broadcast's different episodes are modeled loosely (and satirically) on various characters and elements from Voltaire's *Candide*. The dean is a version of Pangloss; the larger-than-life, bombastic, and egotistical music professor that shows up in the second episode is named Maestro Tronkh; the featured guest of the third episode is a professor named Martin, an educator who was once enthusiastic about and inspired in his teaching, but who is now just marking time until his retirement.

The penultimate episode features a student named Mauve. She's not named for any character from *Candide*, so we can't mistake her for a caricature. She is a member of a student group (she refuses the term "leader," insisting instead that the group is a "non-hierarchical society") that describes itself like this on the radio broadcast:

> "This is a message of warning. ... We stand as a front united against the tyranny of all authority. Rise up, students, and weaponize your anger for a cause that doesn't pretend to stand for anything. The 'representation' that is our student government is a patronizing façade. Skip your classes. Trash your dorms. Vandalize. We are more than collective bargaining. We are the end of all things as you know it. Meetings are held on Sundays at midnight at the Student Union. Free pizza."

In this satirical space, it's easy to see the makings of the explosive campus dynamics that Greg Lukianoff and Jonathan Haidt describe in their book, *The Coddling of the American Mind*. On the one side there are students who are exasperated with faculty and one another for their ham-fisted, archaic, and ineffective grasp of the intricate identity politics accosting these elite spaces. These students are responding to and reciprocating the antagonism and condescension that they feel on a gut level directed at them by faculty and administration. And on the other side is a faculty and administration that are too narrowly focused on their own pet interests and the college's bottom line to create spaces of community and actual learning, too enamored of the sound of their own voices to listen to the voices of their students.

The thesis captures what we'd like to call the "hypocrisy-cynicism complex" that we fear forms the current culture of so many SLACs, the toxic distrust flowing from the top down and then all the way back up again. This complex includes the perceptions and biases with which people at SLACs too often approach one another: the suspicion (too often borne out) that administrators make decisions on a cost-cutting, rather than a pedagogical, basis, that time and resource-draining strategic plans are determined from the start, that the drastic and inhumane cuts across many college campuses are simply the result of the inscrutable visions of trustees, that students are just there for a piece of paper and don't care about learning for its own sake. At a large number of campuses around the country, benefit of the doubt and goodwill are in rather short supply. SLACs say they want to be one kind of institution— places that nurture a love of learning, places that produce good and kind citizens, leaders, and entrepreneurs. They profess to value diversity and inclusion, equity, accessibility, risk-taking, and critical thinking. But they don't enact these values. The students know it. We know it. And so, hypocrisy breeds cynicism, and it all undermines what we're really here to do.

The thesis begins with this passage, the first of several reworkings of Nietzsche's famous "eternal return" parable:

> Imagine yourself in your loneliest loneliness. Aren't you tired by now? Tired of bad faith? Tired of the same lies, repeated over and over? I'm not talking about lies like "'I'm so sorry I couldn't make it to class, I was feeling sick," or, "Why yes, I *am* proficient in Microsoft Excel." I'm talking about lies that kill truth. Lies that have existed forever

and have been spoken so long that they've become the new reality. Maybe you're aware of these lies; but actually realizing their exposure would be so devastating that you'd rather be complicit and miserable. It'd be nice if we could take up arms, wouldn't it?

So many of us who teach at small liberal arts colleges *are* tired of bad faith, of the lies that have become the new reality. But we also share the extraordinary sense of loss that being ripped from our campuses represents. It's a deeply ambivalent space, to feel both the promise of the residential model—to have experienced the magic that can and does happen on these campuses where people are living and learning together—and the profound disappointment that we're not living up to our full potential. Not by a long shot.

Chain-Sickness

Before the shutdown, when this student came to talk with me about their thesis, it was because they were feeling a sense of resignation and dissatisfaction with the writing of the thing, a sense of being hemmed in by the conventions of the process to produce something that fit neatly into disciplinary boxes in ways they didn't want to have to make them fit. They were right to feel this way. The thesis defense meeting made clear that the other members of the committee were expecting something far more conventional. They had trouble entering into the world this student had created, despite its bearing such a resemblance to our own, and despite its capacity to provide lessons for how we might address the toxic culture in which we find ourselves. On this side of the shutdown, through the lens of that push and pull between passion and its dampening, this student was more clearly able to articulate the source of that resignation and dissatisfaction. The student described it as the "apathetic masochism" of higher education. "We're taught to be embarrassed about our love for our subject," they protested:

> We're taught that we are supposed to put meaning and joy aside in the pursuit of 'knowledge.' What I most wish I had experienced in college was a full-on commitment to the mission. ... I keep thinking about what will need to happen for everything to come to a stop. I don't WANT school to end, I really don't think most people should have another line cut off. It reminds me about Nietzsche's chain-sickness. At this moment, I think chain-sickness is better for my authenticity than loneliness.

This description resonates with us and serves as a touchstone for our manifesto. Nietzsche's concept of chain-sickness—the collective paralysis and resentment, and the crystallization and reiteration of so many practices of our own devising that are making us *sick*—provides a perfect framework. Chain-sickness grows out of the self-deception that the values and institutions that *we have created* are somehow given and necessary, eternal and transcendent. It festers when we forget that we have the power to change our values, when we view ourselves as powerless beings subject to forces outside of our control. The fictitious dean of the thesis points to the symptoms, as she sees it, of this condition: "[The students] meander about campus like sedated livestock; they refuse to do their academics, they overindulge each and every weekend just to make it through the next slog of a week! The students are *sick*." In true-to-character, one-dimensional fashion, the dean places full blame on the students, lacking the larger awareness of how these symptoms reflect the manifold ways in which the system has broken down. Even so, the multipronged accusation has more than a little merit, as those of us teaching in SLACs can attest. "Work hard, play hard" has become something of a mantra, a catchall phrase used to brush aside the insidious heavy-drinking culture and its fallout—deaths, assaults, sexual assaults, date rapes—so prevalent on these campuses (National Institute on Alcohol Abuse and Alcoholism), not to mention the fatigue, that sense of slogging through, manifested increasingly in the classroom. Six months before the pandemic, a student described it this way:

> I think this semester I have become particularly bored with the monotony of school. While I have found my courses to be engaging, I have found it to be increasingly more difficult to reach a level of eustress that allows me to be productive and motivated. ... It is not that I am unhappy or sad, but rather I am disconnected from my emotions and have found it difficult to always keep in mind the reason for why I am doing this in the first place. I am 19 years old, and, although I have career goals, I have no idea if that is actually where I will end up or what I will end up loving. While it would be nice to be able to jump straight into a career and figure out right away if it is actually something I am passionate about, our societal structure has made it increasingly difficult to do that. Within today's society, it is critical that I attain an undergraduate degree before I begin learning about what I truly believe myself to be interested in.

This insight is from a student who still managed to create a breathtaking final project, a "This I Believe" statement (modeled on the classic NPR program), built on Tilt Brush, a virtual reality platform, that explored the principles and individual and collective implications of universal design. And yet she captures so stoically this sense of disconnection, the disembodied quality of the thing, the just-going-through-the-motions essence of it all.

This is the chain-sickness. We know our students are engaged, we know that they want to learn, and we know that they have the capacity to produce extraordinary things. We suspect, *à la* Lukianoff and Haidt in *The Coddling of the American Mind*, that a portion of the growing sense of fatigue in the classroom can be chalked up to the substantial identity politics often provoked on predominantly white campuses with a heavy Greek presence, such as DePauw's, and to the sharp rise in mental health issues so many of our students are facing. Certainly, too, a good bit of it has to do with the vast range of learning styles, learning goals, and intended paths for life after graduation that are represented in any given course.

But much of it, we're convinced, has to be attributed to the ratcheting up of the high-stakes testing culture that our students have been subjected to since kindergarten and the data-driven, assessment-and-outcomes-crazed, "college and career readiness" mentality that has overtaken education as a whole. Our students are collectively burnt out. We have burned them out. So all this talk about "student-centeredness" means nothing if we don't hear what our students are telling us, if we don't *listen* to what it has felt like for them to have been told for thirteen years that they are primarily valuable as data points, as cogs in a wheel, as a means to a bottom line. We reiterate this message every time we sell their successes on our websites, every time we shape the narrative of success along normative lines, and every time we tell students how they need to master the narrow subset of knowledge we have deemed most important for them to know.

The title of the student's thesis we keep returning to

resonates particularly in this context: "Become What You Are: The Student Handbook to Fighting Nihilism." From kindergarten on up, our students have been told who to be and how to be, how to learn and what to learn. It is so rare for us to say that the task of higher education is to help students become who they are. Authenticity. It's a clichéd term, perhaps as empty as "student-centered" in this self-help-saturated cultural moment in which we live. But so much of the brokenness, so much of the toxicity of the culture we don't want to return to, is, we believe, a function of students who are not being authentically encouraged to become who they are, and of institutions that do not have the vision to become what they truly are.

As this student describes it, overcoming chain-sickness involves committing fully to a mission rather than succumbing to the "apathetic masochism" that these institutions tend to breed, despite their stated intentions. We think so, too. And we return to the email exchange between the DePauw student and the VPAA, which demonstrates with a raw clarity the pain of this chain-sickness, this sense, fueled perhaps by resignation, that the system we have created must necessarily continue in the same fashion, even if there are no good solutions. It's the sense of being locked in. And as we see it, the Janus-faced nature of this moment of crisis presents a call to action for SLACs: to turn that chain-sickness into health.

PART TWO

THIS REALLY ISN'T WORKING

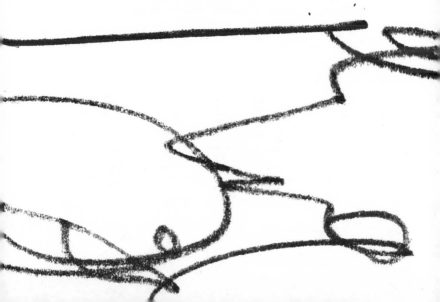

The email exchange between the DePauw senior, sheltering-in-place after his campus closed, and his college's VPAA has a classically *tragic* feel to it. There are no obvious "bad guys" here, neither "coddled" students nor callous administrators. Rather, both correspondents inhabit a culture, a way-of-being, that they clearly esteem, but which is generating dreadful results for them. As such, it indicates the deep fissures, pandemic-related or not, in higher education. We are in crisis.

The media often point to Louisiana State University's "lazy river" as the most glaring expression of higher education's broken state and misguided priorities. The "river" in question, part of an $85 million refurbishment of LSU's recreation center, is a stream fashioned into the university's initials that students can gently float down on inner tubes. But why pour so much money into a sumptuous waterway when, to cite just one failing, LSU's student-faculty ratio is considerably higher than the national average? Is it perhaps, as a reporter for the *Chronicle of Higher Education* observed, because administrators feel obliged "to service the whims and desires of tuition-paying students, whose satisfaction has become ever more crucial as state support wanes" (Stripling)?

In the language of economics, demand-side market pressure "may compel investment in consumption amenities rather than academic quality at many institutions" (Jacob et al. 311). A member of LSU's board was a bit clearer: "It's first class, yeah. But nowadays you've got to have it."

For some years now, prioritizing "consumption amenities" has meant sacrificing learning on the altar of luxury. To cite a more common example than LSU's lazy river, many parents, eager that college residences will afford the same comforts of home, want their children to live in apartment-style housing and single rooms. Colleges have responded accordingly, even though research indicates that students in such residences are less likely to succeed academically than those living in traditional dorm spaces where making friends is a greater possibility, a key component of student success (Brown et al.).

What lazy rivers and single dorm rooms suggest is not that higher education has *become* a business. That ship sailed long ago. Rather, the problem, as Victor E. Ferrall Jr. observes, is in determining whether colleges are sellers or buyers in this particular marketplace. It's hard to maintain that higher education sells "learning," for example, although we expect our graduates to know more, and hopefully be wiser, at the end of their time with us. But we lack a way to measure what was learned, even though the grades we assign act as a proxy for learning. More cynically, many critics have argued that higher education actually sells credentials, "a piece of paper that would translate my expertise to employer terms," as one student put it (Cottom 2018). In this prestige economy, it is only to be expected that a Harvard degree will cost more than the one on offer from Montana State University, since the former is "worth more" than the latter in terms of what it can "buy" once a graduate is out in the real world. If this assessment is accurate, it is a deeply disturbing problem for most of us who work in higher education, from instructors to presidents, because we actually care deeply about student learning and want to ensure that our graduates have the best possible shot at success, *however* we define it.

What the increasing attention to amenities actually indicates is that higher education is as much in the business of *buying* students as it is in the business of *selling* an education (Ferrall 64). Whether the student-age population is decreasing, as is currently the case, or increasing, more than 4,000 institutions of higher education across the United States are competing for students in a market that lavishly rewards those who are deemed "winners" and punishes those who are deemed "losers." And as the scramble for personal protective equipment by states during the pandemic has revealed, when competition replaces collaboration, the losers far outnumber the winners. In the marketplace for students, the winners are those who have their pick of high school graduates. They are the colleges and universities that can vacuum up those deemed the "brightest" *and* those whose families can afford the full sticker price, not to mention those who will likely contribute to the school's already substantial endowment far into the future.

The wealthiest private institutions compete to buy students with generous aid offers to the small percentage of them who cannot afford the costs, with the promise of robust alumni networks, and with the potential for high-income employment upon graduation. The next tier of private colleges will try to entice "top-flight" students away from offers at Stanford or the Ivies with attractive merit scholarships, even though the families of those students could afford to shoulder the full tuition. Some colleges market their location as an added incentive to undecided student consumers. One private college in southern California, with a commanding view of the Pacific, sends admitted students logo-emblazoned beach towels and invites them to campus where they can feast on food from In-N-Out Burger trucks that are brought in for the occasion. The promise of a set of socket wrenches offered to my (Steve's) son as an inducement for enrolling in a nearby mechanics college is not likely to compete. Flagship state universities market their sports teams, Greek life, and in-state tuition in order to fill as many desks as possible, since the state support they receive is determined by the number of students they enroll. Regional public institutions and community colleges compete for students, and the public dollars they bring, by virtue of location and price. And for-profits desperately (and often dishonestly) soak up federal funds by marketing themselves to veterans or Pell-eligible students.

But wait, we hope you will counter, aren't we forgetting something? What about the strength of the educational program, the quality of the faculty, the boundless resources that the top-tier institutions pour into their students? To be sure. Both Beth and I come from colleges with great libraries, science labs, music facilities, and superb and committed faculty. And we'd like to think that students choose to attend our schools because of those qualities. But, in reality, they know more about our schools' reputations than they know about *us*, the faculty: how much time we will devote to each of them, and whether we are engaging teachers as well as published scholars. More to the point, though, exceptional teachers can be found literally everywhere, at every school. Faculty at Glendale Community College, for example, are just as committed to making a positive impact on the lives of their students as those in the Ivies, and they do so with far fewer resources.

Almost every one of us who enters the world of higher education, as faculty, administrators, or staff, do so because we love our calling, not because of the big bucks we are (un) likely to earn. But as we view the competition that schools find themselves in as they scramble to buy students, the feeling only grows that something is not working. This only became clearer when the semester ground to a halt with the COVID-19 shutdown. If the academic dean at DePauw could not provide a solution to his student's anguish, it's not because he didn't want to. And it's not even because he, like the rest of us, lacked answers to an unprecedented crisis. Something had stopped working *before* the crisis brought it into sharp relief. Wittingly or unwittingly, we have become part of a process that has turned students into commodities whose value is determined by the colleges who bid for them. And all the lazy rivers in the world will not repair that. But, if we *are* to fix the problem, we need to know what is broken, what went wrong, and why things just aren't working as they should.

The Rise of Inequality

To do this, there is no better starting point than these statistics: Gross Domestic Product, a measure of a country's total economic output, has risen in the United States almost 80 percent since 1979 (adjusting for inflation and population growth), an average of some 2 percent per year. In that period, the income of the bottom half of wage earners has gone up just 20 percent. Those in the middle 40 percent have seen their income boosted by half, and those at the top, the highest .01 percent of wage earners, have seen their incomes rocket up some 420 percent. Let the good times roll.

On average, each of these top income earners now accumulates just shy of $20 million a year. And that's income, not overall net worth. The top .01 percent of all households now own more than 11 percent of all the wealth in the United States while the net worth of the median American household was actually about 30 percent *lower* in 2016 than it was in 2007. (The numbers are even more jaw-dropping for the world as a whole, where, in 2019, twenty-six *people* were estimated to own as much as the poorest 3.8 *billion people* combined) (Elliott). The COVID-19 pandemic is only accelerating this trend. According to one study, the combined wealth of America's billionaires increased by $282 billion in the *three weeks* between March 18 and April 10, 2020, while unemployment surged (Collins et al.). Goldman Sachs, the investment banking and financial services firm, reported its second highest net revenues ever in the second quarter of 2020, the epicenter of the pandemic earthquake.

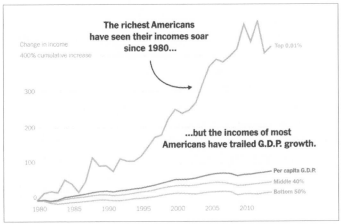

GDP and After Tax Income Growth by Income Sector, 1980-2014

As income disparity has grown, the chasm between the total assets owned by white and Black people has also widened to an astonishing degree. According to new research, the average Black family with children holds one penny of wealth for every dollar that the average white family with children holds (Percheski and Gibson-Davis). And let's be perfectly clear: this widening gap doesn't just mean that the rich own more stuff than the poor. It means that, *on average*, the wealthy can be expected to live an average of thirteen years longer than the poor, even if they reside in the same city

(Tavernise and Sun). In Chicago, residents of West Garfield Park (predominantly Black and poor) have a life expectancy of sixty-nine years; for those on the Near North Side (white and rich), they can look forward on average to eighty-five years. Near North Siders can expect to see their grandkids grow into adulthood; not so much those in West Garfield Park. The pandemic has pulled the curtain even further back on the racial and class divides that continue to define the United States. COVID-19 is killing African Americans at almost three times the rate of white people.

While the US economy has always generated both wealth and poverty, the magnitude of the inequality produced over the last forty years is extraordinary, particularly when compared with the period between 1945 and 1980. In the immediate postwar years, the economy reflected a Keynesian ("Fordist" or demand-side) consensus characterized by industrial growth and reasonable wages, a stable (sometimes compliant) union movement that was accepted as a reliable bargaining partner, the expansion of a modest social welfare net, and state intervention via a more progressive fiscal policy that taxed high incomes. Corporations described their own (modest) form of social responsibility. As late as 1980, the Business Roundtable argued that corporations "have a responsibility, first of all, to make available to the public quality goods and services at fair prices, thereby earning a profit that attracts investment to continue and enhance the enterprise, provide jobs and build the economy" (Gomory and Sylla 107). But that model had already come under attack. "There is one and only one social responsibility of business," the economist Milton Friedman insisted in 1970, "to use its resources and engage in activities designed to increase its profits."

The fundamental reorientation of the nation's political economy, which would undermine the Keynesian consensus, was termed *neoliberalism*, and it began in earnest with the election of Ronald Reagan in the United States and rise of Margaret Thatcher in the United Kingdom (Harvey, Stiglitz). As a form of economic organization, neoliberalism is characterized by the state's retreat from meaningful forms of regulation, an incessant drive to lower taxes on the wealthy, the privatization of public resources, an emphasis on financial capital over industrial capital, the removal of almost all barriers to private capital accumulation, and a corporate focus on shareholder value above all else. As the accumulation of private wealth became a coveted outcome, rationalized by the argument that a rising tide lifts all boats, the government reduced taxes on the wealthy and corporations, treated social needs as an inconvenience, and saw wage increases as an impediment to the United States' ability to compete internationally. In 1965, compensation for CEOs at the 350 largest companies in the United States by sales was about twenty times greater than that of the average employee. Now, in the wake of decades of neoliberal economic policy, it is about three hundred times larger. And that figure is even higher for the superrich. The CEO of McDonald's, for example, earns 2,124 times the wage of the corporation's median-paid employee (Wiles).

As a political program, neoliberalism has tunneled under the liberal democratic state, gutting labor unions, suppressing access to the ballot, and crafting a gerrymandered electoral system in which legislators choose their voters rather than the other way around. The Supreme Court has expedited the strangulation of democratic safeguards by gifting corporations with rights previously held only by citizens, a move which unleashed a flood of money that has swamped the electoral system. Workers, for their part, have been removed from stable jobs that provide benefits and have been thrust instead into the gig economy, where they drive Ubers, run packages around Amazon warehouses, or race from campus to campus to teach classes.

As an ideology, neoliberalism elevates economic choices above all others while subordinating social concerns to an "I'll take care of mine" mentality. Wealthy voters in one town who refused tax increases that would have kept streetlights on in all parts of the city instead spent even more on an "Adopt a Light" program to insure that their blocks would not be left in the dark. Private property rights trump any notion of the public good. In a 1987 interview, Margaret Thatcher famously remarked, "There's no such thing as society ... people must look after themselves first." Her words echoed the libertarian icon, Ayn Rand, who wrote in 1941, "The right to liberty means man's right to individual action, individual choice, individual initiative and individual property. Without the right to private property no independent action is possible" (Sunstein 34). Those without property, including African Americans who have been denied property ownership by centuries of slavery, terror, redlining, and other racist practices, and the nearly 90 percent of the population—both Black and white—who don't have enough for retirement, are written off as failures, "takers" not "makers," or losers who deserve any suffering that befalls them.

In this sense, neoliberalism's all-consuming focus on the market and property ownership has served to reinforce older rationalizations for racism in the United States, which has generated the current crisis expressed in the Black Lives Matter movement. Under neoliberalism, the "market" presents itself as a neutral agency that will reward anyone with "grit" and intelligence. The American dream of homeownership, the reasoning goes, offers itself to those who work hard enough. People of color, however, and Black people specifically, have deliberately and expressly been denied access to both the market and property. "The world around us," Hilton Als wrote of the police riot in Brownsville, Brooklyn, in 1967, "was not the one we had worked hard to achieve but the quiet, degraded world that our not-country said we deserved. We couldn't keep nothing, the elders said, not even ourselves" (20). Lacking property, they have been found responsible for their own poverty. This ideology, backed by government policy and state power, has pushed the country toward higher degrees of racial segregation than there were during the Jim Crow era (Rothstein).

Neoliberal ideology has maintained and enforced racism. By turning over ethical decision-making to the "market," it has likewise distorted the liberal concept of freedom. Isaiah Berlin argued that there are two modes of freedom, negative and positive: freedom *from* and freedom *to*. Under neoliberalism, *freedom from constraint* has become the right to accumulate wealth unfettered by all regulation and animated by the thought that every dollar accumulated by the makers is nothing short of heroic. In contrast, Berlin writes that positive freedom, the freedom *to*, is a "wish, above all, to be conscious of myself as a thinking, willing, active being, bearing responsibility for my choices and able to explain them by references to my own ideas and purposes." Under neoliberalism, the freedom to act has been untethered from the need to act responsibly or even rationally. It is deeply ironic, if not tragic, that neoliberalism's self-serving definition of "freedom," constructed with only the wealthiest in mind, has been absorbed and is now enacted by a populist base that has been impoverished and driven to unforeseen levels of despair by this very same economic model. The degree to which we have spun into a neoliberal rabbit hole was starkly revealed during the pandemic by protesters who demanded that their states, and their bodies, be "liberated" from the tyrannical, health-related shutdowns imposed by some governors. "Give me Liberty or Give Me COVID-19," they implored.

sm and Higher Education

cation has hardly been exempt from the impact alism, even though colleges and universities are often criticized for sheltering their students from "the real world," spoiling them rather than toughening them up for what awaits. "Our universities are doing students a disservice by coddling them," Karin Agness Lips wrote in *Forbes*, employing Lukianoff and Haidt's sour term. "They won't be prepared for post-graduation life." Her desire to make college more of a boot camp, and less the summer camp she imagines it to be, overlooks the fact that fewer than a fifth of today's students are "traditional"; that is, full-time students who live on campus and who are between eighteen and twenty-two years old. The other 80 percent don't have to be reminded about what the "real" world entails, about the jobs they work, the children they raise, or the parents they care for while getting a degree. Far from being removed from the "real" world, higher education has been stamped by it. And it is for this reason that, when advocating for a radical reimagining of the small liberal arts college, we acknowledge that, in many ways, this entails a broader political challenge, a willingness to dismantle the larger societal structures that uphold economic inequality and racial injustice.

Higher Education and the Inequalities of K–12 Education

Consider how four events from the 1970s have shaped the unjust nature of K–12 schooling in the United States.

First, in *San Antonio Independent School District v. Rodriguez* (1973), a sharply divided Supreme Court ruled (5–4) that there was no constitutional right to equal funding for public K–12 education. Since public education has always been funded largely through local property taxes, wealthier school districts have always spent substantially more per student than poorer districts. In 1973, by one vote, the Supreme Court argued that there could be no federal mandate for educational equity. Poorer communities would suffer from poorly resourced schools.

Then, the following year, in *Milliken v. Bradley*, with the same 5–4 split, the Court quashed a Detroit-area busing plan designed to address the city's highly segregated public schools. In effect, the court determined that millions of children condemned by residential segregation to under-resourced schools would not be allowed to access schools in nearby wealthier districts, perpetuating, as Justice Thurgood Marshall wrote, "the very evil that *Brown* [*v. Board of Education*] was aimed at" ending (Turner et al. 3).

An anti-tax revolt launched in 1978 in California with the passage of Proposition 13 signaled that, particularly when faced with a growing number of students of color, states and localities would move to starve public education of necessary funding. By lowering property taxes, they further weakened public school systems in low-income areas and hastened the exodus of wealthier (largely white) parents from public to private schools.

Finally, the charter school movement, first proposed in the mid-1970s and implemented in the 1990s, allowed public tax dollars to follow children out of resource-starved schools to new, private charter schools. By 2018, three-quarters of the students in New York City's public schools qualified for free or reduced-priced lunches and less than 10 percent were white (Algar); 86 percent of students in Detroit were from low-income families and less than 3 percent were white (Catolico). Currently, a poor child in a poor district in a poor state receives about $8,000 per year worth of schooling; the figure for rich children in rich states is $18,000. And for very rich children in elite private schools, it can be as much as $75,000. The privatization of K–12 education has meant that, for many, if you want a quality education, you have to pay for it (Markovits 128).

Neoliberalism and the Undermining of the "Public Good"

The shift away from public support for education is one example of how, under neoliberalism, private gain has crowded out any concept of a "public good." For economists, "public goods" are things that are "non-rivalrous" and "non-excludable." "Non-rivalrous" means that my use of a public good doesn't reduce your ability to access it. "Non-excludability" means that it's virtually impossible to deny anyone the benefits of the good. Public parks or clean air are public goods, for example—or at least they used to be. Prosperity in the United States in years following World War II (at least for whites) was underwritten by a capacious understanding of the public good. That included quality public K–12 schools, universities, and libraries, not to mention investments in infrastructure and mass transit. But even as federal and state budgets have grown over the past half century, the share of national wealth spent on public goods has not. As cities and states have reduced taxes on the wealthy, the goods and services which they previously supported—things like streetlights, public parks, and fire departments—have been absorbed by private companies and made available for a fee, or not at all.

Higher education is another such public good that has been subverted by neoliberal policies. Furthermore, as states reduced funding for higher education, and as higher education itself came to be viewed through a partisan lens, the public found fewer reasons to support it. A Pew Research survey from 2017 found that only 36 percent of Republicans and independents thought that colleges and universities had a positive effect on the country (Fingerhut). An equally meager percentage of all US adults expressed confidence in K–12 public schools, down from 58 percent in 1973 (Calderon et al.). The deterioration of support for public K–12 schooling has impacted communities of color—which have *always* suffered from a disproportionate lack of educational resources—with particular intensity. In April 2020, the Court of Appeals for the Sixth Circuit ruled that the state of Michigan had been so negligent toward the educational needs of Detroit's students that children had been "deprived of access to literacy" in violation of the Fourteenth Amendment.

Eroding the Ability to Pay for Higher Education

Over the past four decades, the cost of higher education has also increased substantially at both private and public universities, even more so since 2000. Tuition and fees at *public* universities have more than doubled (in constant dollars) over the last thirty years, and they are increasing at a faster rate than those at private universities (Tuition). Why they have gone up should not be surprising given what we've described about K–12 funding: legislators not only are reluctant to fund higher education, but they also find it is one of the easiest budget items to cut. One study estimates that in the first decade of the twenty-first century, almost 80 percent of tuition hikes at public universities were linked to a decline in state appropriations (Hiltonsmith 1). Ten years ago, students and their families paid for about a third of a university's operating costs through tuition and fees; now they must cover nearly half those costs. There is more to be said about the substantial rise in the price of private colleges and universities, and we will address that in part 3. But one important element in the conversation about college affordability is often absent. If the cost of higher education has increased, the ability of middle-income families to afford it has declined because their salaries and wages have remained almost stagnant for *forty years*. The purchasing power of the federal minimum wage peaked in 1968; it's been falling ever since. If individual incomes had kept pace with the country's overall economic growth since 1970, those in the bottom *90 percent* of the income distribution would be making, on average, an extra $12,000 per year (Editorial Board). The average tuition at four-year public colleges rose by a little more than $14,000 (in constant dollars) over the last thirty years. What should have been a small gap between the cost of higher education and a family's ability to afford it has become a vast chasm that has been filled instead by $1.56 trillion in student loans. And, not surprisingly, Black families bear more of this burden. Four out of five African Americans graduate college with debt; on average they carry 70 percent more debt than white students (Cottom 2018).

Ranking Systems, the Benchmark of Meritocracy, and Upended Values

Each year, the college football ranking system generates endless debates about which team is actually the best, and how one should determine who gets to face off in the national championship. Things are not so simple when ranking colleges as a whole, but the entities that are in the business of generating national collegiate ranking schemes have grown fat, even as they have seriously distorted higher education. Facing declining revenues as a news magazine, *U.S. News & World Report* introduced its first college ranking issue in 1983. It proved to be a smart move for them, although higher education has suffered the consequences. Ranking systems soon became an immensely powerful juggernaut, feeding, as they do, middle-class parents' concerns about their children's ability to make it in the world, and elite desires to retain privilege and power. One can now find rankings based on everything from the number of graduates who become venture capitalists (the University Entrepreneur Report), to schools considered "dream colleges" by students and parents (the Princeton Review). Publications rank colleges on the basis of "value for money," the starting salaries earned by graduates, and the number of students in the Peace Corps or other forms of community-involved work.

Leaving aside the questionable validity or reliability of any of these schemes, it is clear that the ranking regime, particularly the one published by *U.S. News & World Report*, has had an inordinate and negative impact on higher education. It has influenced decisions by students and parents about where to apply, decisions that are often largely driven by the desire to accumulate social capital, since students can obtain an excellent education at hundreds and hundreds of universities, and not just at the forty or so colleges that admit fewer than 20 percent of their applicants. But more profoundly, rankings have also been used by institutions to determine where to allocate their own scarce resources. As one study noted, rankings "influence institutions' strategic positioning and planning, staffing and organization, quality assurance, resource allocation and fundraising, and admissions and financial aid" (Espinosa et al. 7). As the former chancellor of the University of North Carolina-Chapel Hill sadly observed, "To any logical scientific observer, the fine distinctions of where schools show up on this list are statistically meaningless—but try telling that to a roomful of alumni or parents. Countless hours of trustee meetings are spent going over the minute details of the formula and setting institutional goals" (Thorp).

By placing a high value on certain metrics—the "admit rate," for example—ranking systems have led colleges to make decisions that would otherwise seem nonsensical, if not downright scandalous. Year after year, resources are deployed to increase the total number of students who submit applications. This is not undertaken to fill the freshman class, but solely in order to *reject* more applicants and thereby lower the school's "admit rate." Do this correctly, and perhaps a school can be elevated from the ranks of (merely) "selective" colleges to the exalted "highly selective" category. Maybe an institution can even become one of only seventeen US colleges that admit less than 10 percent of their applicants (Desilver). Think of all the hearts it'll be able to break then! (One March day, I—Steve—watched in dismay as my neighbor's son set fire to a sweatshirt from his most desired college, the one that had just sent him a rejection notice.)

This is a process that is put on auto-repeat year after year. After moving into the top fifty colleges in *U.S. News*'s rankings, according to one study, institutions saw their admit rate decline and their ability to attract high school students in the top 10 percent of their graduating class increase (Bowman and Bastedo). Between 2002 and 2017, the most selective schools (those that reject more than 90 percent of all applicants while enrolling less than 4 percent of all students), saw their applications double. They increased their selectivity even further in this spiraling competition by admitting 8 percent *fewer* students over that period. Fallout from the college ranking systems has cascaded backward, generating a deranged competition for placement in the "best" (i.e., the most exclusive) schools that now stretches back to preschool, where the most competitive admit fewer than 10 percent of their applicants (Dhingra). About 30,000 students in New York City, for example, compete for the 4,000 openings each year at one of the city's eight elite public high schools. This so-called meritocratic ranking system produces extreme levels of anxiety and alienation among students; because it operates within the structures of systemic racism, it also generates outcomes that should surprise no one. In 2020, only ten Black students, out of a freshman class of roughly 760, were admitted to Stuyvesant, a highly regarded selective public high school in New York City. The more that higher education is driven by the false meritocracy embedded in the ranking system, the more distorted it becomes, replacing the value of learning with the potential of earning, reinforcing the sense of privilege absorbed by the "winners," and generating the grotesque behaviors on display in the admissions scandal of 2019 (Medina et al.).

Higher Education as an Engine of Inequality

Some colleges and universities with very large endowments offer low-income students a "free ride" (no tuition, room, or board). Most schools, however, aren't capable of such generosity. Low-income students find themselves blocked from many institutions of higher education because they can't afford them, because the inequity baked into the structures of K–12 education has deprived them of the quality education that could have prepared them for admission, or because they were discouraged from applying in the first place. When combined with other factors that favor the wealthy (including "legacy" and donor-linked admissions), the current admissions system ultimately produces elite colleges and universities that are, well, elite. Less than 5 percent of Ivy League students, for example, come from the bottom 20 percent of the income distribution (Nova and Schoen). At many selective colleges, there are more students from the top 1 percent of income than from the bottom 60 percent. This income stratification replicates itself, generation after generation, determining that wealthy schools continue to build on their wealth. The forty colleges and universities with the largest endowments, led by Harvard, hold more than two-thirds of all the wealth among the 500 most financially stable colleges, and this is not even mentioning the 3,500 others whose economic futures are insecure (Woodhouse). Simply put, higher education, which was intended to spur mobility, has become a platform for reproducing and reinforcing inequality.

It is already clear that the COVID-19 crisis will further trim the ranks of low-income students at institutions of higher learning. At a moment when requests for federal aid should be *increasing*, given the dramatic rise in unemployment, data from April 2020 show an 8 percent decline in aid requests among current college students with annual family incomes below $25,000, as well as a sizable decrease in requests for aid filed by high school seniors. Both are signs that low-income students are abandoning higher education, forced out by the economic crisis.

Higher Education and the Gig Economy

Neoliberalism's relentless push to reduce labor costs has given rise to the so-called "gig economy" in which workers are displaced from permanent jobs with benefits and at least some protections, and forced to accept short-term contracts or freelance work, which offer neither benefits nor stability. This is the "Uber economy," populated by contract programmers, delivery drivers, and dog walkers. And it has absorbed a large part of the academic sector as well. If we have some concerns with the tenure system, which we will raise in the next section, at least it was originally designed to protect academic freedom, provide continuous employment, suggest a stable set of expectations, and offer reasonable compensation. The same cannot be said for higher education's current system of contingent hiring. In 1970, roughly three-fourths of all faculty were either tenured or on the tenure track (Schuster and Finkelstein 41). As of 2017, though, only a third of faculty were tenured or on the tenure track. The rest were adjuncts, the "fast food workers" of the academic world.

Adjunct faculty pick up courses where they can, often at more than one institution, receive little or no benefits, and serve at the pleasure of the institution. For adjuncts, life is not easy; 65 percent of them earn less than $50,000 a year. The story of James Hoff, an English PhD, is not atypical. Hoff taught four courses a semester for the princely sum of $24,000 a year, which is slightly above the poverty level (Swarns). Most adjuncts earn between $2,500 and $4,000 per course. At the same time, the median salary of a chief academic officer in 2019 was about $400,000 at private doctoral institutions; that of presidents was just shy of $700,000. The exact same forces that have widened the gap between wage workers and CEOs in the private sector are on display in the academy (Chronicle 40).

The Student as Customer

Not long ago, a colleague at a nearby university was taken aside by her department chair in the middle of the semester after some students complained that her grading was too demanding. She was informed that she would be "relieved" of the course. When the same thing happened to another professor the following semester, my colleague took the issue to her dean. He commiserated, but observed that there wasn't much that could be done. The university was, after all, part of "a consumer culture." The student-as-customer, a prominent signpost along the neoliberal highway, takes us back to the *cri de coeur* with which we began: higher education just isn't working for anyone. If education has become a marketplace where customers shop for what they want and rely on administrators to back them up, the faculty has lost its hard-won professionalism, not to mention its authority, in the educational system. On the other hand, if the faculty treat their students as whiners who are always looking to "get away with something," then students have lost their right to have an important voice in their own learning. "Sorry, kids, you are not the authority in the classroom," one grumpy educator commented in response to a *New York Times* op-ed about student evaluations of faculty. "Me Teacher. You student. Me Teach, you learn. End of discussion. ... You are not my customer. My classroom is not Burger King. You do not get to 'have it your way'" (Pritscher 103).

A model that elevates grievance and suspicion and places administrators in the role of customer service representatives cannot cultivate learning. The neoliberal, market model, as Miguel Martinez-Saenz and Steven Schoonover, Jr. have observed, has encouraged the "false idea that the consumer alone can adequately speak in the name of education. Students cannot hope to do this [alone]. But neither can the administration or the faculty." What remains is a system in which no one is left to speak in the name of education. "We must recognize," they conclude, "that the only way to speak on behalf of universal educational interests is to find ways of speaking—each group from its distinct position—as a single voice" (Martinez-Saenz and Schoonover Jr.).

SLACs and the Economy of Self-Interest

In 2019, some two million students graduated with bachelor's degrees, along with more than one million who earned associate's degrees or certificates. They took classes at more than 4,000 institutions of postsecondary education, studying everything from cosmetology to computer engineering. They sat in classes whose average size ranged from less than a dozen to the thousands, interacting intimately with classmates in person or at a distance via computer screens. Some lived in dorms, ate in dining halls, played lacrosse, wrote for the school paper, and laid out $70,000 a year; others commuted to campus, ate lunch from Tupperware containers, and crammed in six courses a semester while holding down a full-time job in order to scrape together the $7,000 in tuition and fees needed to bring them a year closer to the diploma they coveted.

Among these institutions, small liberal arts colleges have offered a distinctive approach to higher education in the United States for over 200 years. Liberal arts colleges are small (usually ranging from a few hundred students to 3,000), primarily undergraduate, residential, and most often located in nonurban areas. Their physical characteristics, when fully utilized, allow for the immersive engagement of teachers with students, and students with their peers, the broader campus community, the off-campus community, and themselves (through reflective practices). Ideally, these characteristics also offer the faculty more opportunities to engage with colleagues outside their own area of expertise, to interact with students in a variety of (nonclassroom) settings, and to establish strong, often residential, ties to the local community. It is through mobilizing these multiple opportunities for engagement that SLACs can offer their "signature pedagogy" (Chick et al.). Small size and residential life facilitate the faculty's ability to know their students as individuals, allow classroom debates to spill over to dorms and dining halls, and enable learning to extend out to the community. Socrates didn't contend with cafeteria food or worry whether or not he would make the basketball team, but his model of engaged questioning established a mode of inquiry-based learning that is more possible in a SLAC than it is in a classroom crammed with 800 students.

Besides being shaped by their physical environment, SLACs are also characterized by the common way they answer three interrelated questions that we address in the manifesto in part 3: What is the purpose of an education? What should students learn? And what pedagogical approaches best contribute to student learning? To suggest that liberal arts colleges are the *only* institutions to frame these questions in this particular fashion is as misleading as suggesting that *all* liberal arts colleges adhere to these approaches. In fact, as we have already suggested, many SLACs have lost sight of the particular role they *can* play in the universe of postsecondary education; they have shifted their priorities to respond to market forces that place the transactional and the search for personal advantage over social considerations. It would be comforting, at least to us, to report that SLACs have resisted the pressures faced by other institutions of higher education to bend the knee to the god of economics above all others. But liberal arts colleges, too, bit by bit, have acceded to the pressure to measure all considerations on a cost-benefit basis. Too frequently, SLACs have promoted an economics of scarcity which fashions them to be players in a zero-sum game, where one person's gain becomes another person's loss: what is won by biology is lost by French; what is added by Amherst is taken from Kenyon. Welcome to the transactional liberal arts college.

In December 2014, Simon Newman, a private equity chief executive with no real experience in higher education, was appointed as president of Mount Saint Mary's University, a Roman Catholic liberal arts institution near Baltimore. Among Newman's early initiatives was a plan to bump up "The Mount's" ranking in *U.S. News* by increasing the first-year retention rate, the percentage of entering students who return for their sophomore year (Volk). The way to do this, he reported in an email to the faculty, was not to actually improve the first-year experience, which would have been a reasonable goal. Rather, his aim was to get "20–25 [weaker] students to leave" at the start of the fall semester, before they would be counted in the reports sent to the ranking agencies.

He planned to send newly arrived first-year students a survey designed to help them "discover more" about themselves (Schisler and Golden). Students were told that the survey was "based on some of the leading thinking in the area of personal motivation," and were asked "to answer as honestly as possible." They were assured that, "there are no wrong answers."

As it turned out, there *were* wrong answers. The survey was not about motivation at all, but was instead an attempt to identify "at risk" first-year students who should be "culled" before the end of September. When the plan was uncovered by senior staff and faculty, Newman responded, "This is hard for you because you think of the students as cuddly bunnies, but you can't. You just have to drown the bunnies ... put a Glock to their heads." Newman resigned in February 2016, after his own wrong answers found their way into the national press.

While the mess at The Mount seemed to revolve around a spectacularly tone-deaf president, what it revealed was actually more troubling, indicative as it was of how the broader trends identified above have passed through the gates of liberal arts colleges as well. When the true intent of the survey was publicized, highlighted by Newman's drowning bunnies analogy, the faculty voted eighty-seven to three for his dismissal. But a poll of students found that more than three-fourths of the 60 percent of students who voted sided with the president. One student even initiated a petition supporting Newman as an "intelligent businessman with only the Mount's best interest at heart," while blasting the faculty for their inability to "embrace much-needed change" (Jaschik 2016). Newman defended those changes, citing everything he had done in his short time on campus, including opening a Starbucks and investing in athletics. He also stressed his desire to shift The Mount away from its traditional liberal arts (and Catholic) orientation. "Catholic doesn't sell," he reportedly informed the faculty, "liberal arts don't sell." What *does* sell, according to Newman, is giving students what employers want—programs in cybersecurity, not French or German (Svrluga).

So much is evident in Newman's own toxic brew: an animus towards students ("Twenty-five percent of our students are dumb and lazy," he once remarked), the relentless undertow of the ranking systems which reshape priorities and encourage the manipulation of statistics, the cynical celebration of the student-as-consumer who is easily placated by Frappuccinos, and the dismissal of faculty as stubborn obstacles to a school's greater profitability. Still, Newman's private equity coarseness only makes it harder to see the problems for what they are. Students are not wrong to demand an education that can help them prepare for the future, but liberal arts colleges have a responsibility to fashion that desire into a broader, more encompassing educational framework rather than turning over the college's priorities to corporate managers. Administrators are not wrong to see faculty as (often) standing in the way of change, but they have to reflect on how their own insincerity and lack of transparency promotes the faculty's shortage of trust. Faculty are not wrong to see the students' demands to teach to their desires as being too self-absorbed, too presentist, or too threatening to ancient legacies, but faculty also need to see these as genuine calls to make teaching and learning more relevant to the moment and to the lives that their students live.

The trends that have structured higher education over the past four decades have widened divisions and created false dichotomies that pit administrators against faculty, faculty against students, and educating for a "life well-lived" against educating for economic survival. We are not naïve about what it will take to remake this system. After all, we are witnessing a train wreck that has been years in the making (Keeling and Hersh, Arum and Roksa).

The spring 2020 closure of colleges and universities due

to the coronavirus pandemic has revealed many of their internal flaws. This is no less true at SLACs than it is at other institutions of higher learning. Many of the problems at small liberal arts colleges arise from their inability or unwillingness to take full advantage of what they have at hand, choosing instead to cling to specific practices and structures that prevent integration, coherence, and collaboration. They arise from the embrace of a scarcity economy which erodes trust and collective identity. They arise from the persistent inability to remove the structures of racial inequality. And they arise from an unwillingness to abandon the *U.S. News* hymnal, which replicates the inequities and injustices of a neoliberal and racist system rather than advancing their own priorities. As Scott Galloway of NYU's Stern School of Business perceptively remarked, "We have become drunk on exclusivity ... we've decided we want to create a set of luxury brands, such that we can continue to offer more to the children of rich people." Taken together, these decisions have engendered practices that many of our students, as well as faculty and administrators, have criticized as hypocritical.

SLACs are exceptionally vulnerable to the "knock on effects" of the pandemic. MacMurray College, a 174-year-old liberal arts college in central Illinois, for example, announced that it was shutting its doors for good in May. "The pandemic squeezed out the last rays of hope," its president lamented. Those who follow academic finances estimate that as many as 20 percent of all small liberal arts colleges are likely to close over the next five years (Zemsky). In such a moment, more than ever before, we cannot afford hypocrisy and the cynicism it generates. Arguments that "we are all in this together" quickly fade when the most vulnerable sectors of our communities are cut loose. Undoubtedly, all academic units will take a hit from the pandemic. But survival will require that we remake our institutions in ways that take advantage of our strengths, allow us to determine our own goals, and defeat the conditions that breed hypocrisy in the first place. If we are truly going to be all in this together, we all need to change.

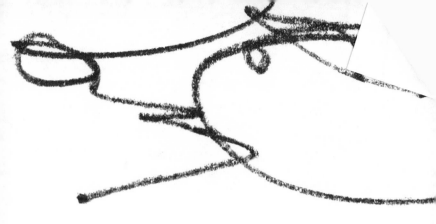

PART THREE

A MANIFESTO: AN INVITATION TO IMAGINE THE POST-PANDEMIC LIBERAL ARTS COLLEGE

"Whatever / contracts keep us social compel us now / to disorder the disorder."
—Claudia Rankine, "Weather"

Some years ago, I (Steve) was invited to consult at a small liberal arts college deep in the throes of a difficult internal reorganization. I planned a series of small meetings with different constituencies as preparation for a daylong workshop with everyone in the same room. Following a frustrating morning session, thick with finger-pointing, I discarded the agenda and instead asked, "If you had your way, how would you change the college?" Everyone had an answer.

I then followed up by asking why they didn't just make the changes they desired. The respondents all said they lacked the power to do so. When I asked who *did* have the power to make change, literally everyone, from the president to the administrative staff, pointed to someone else. Faculty said they were being blocked by the senior administration. Senior administrators said they were being blocked by the faculty. Staff said they were being blocked by both faculty and administrators.

Where does this feeling of powerlessness come from? The

inertia characteristic of many institutions of higher education is often attributed to the fact that different sources of authority (faculty, administrators, trustees, alumni) are either resistant to change or are easily impeded by other powerholders. College presidents aren't corporate CEOs and, besides, they don't stay around all that long (six-and-a-half years is now the average tenure). Trustees are wary of alienating the alumni and tend to be protective of the president they have hired. Faculty, not unreasonably, don't want to give up hard-won privileges and often think more about protecting local (departmental) interests instead of advancing institutional priorities. Institutions that generate suspicion about the motives of other stakeholders are more likely to remain stuck in place, offering scant nibbles around the edges of problems (usually under the hyperbolic label of "strategic planning"), rather than engaging in a serious act of cultural reimagination. Powerlessness, in this context, becomes a rationalization for inertia rather than a cause of it. The question, of course, is why. Why do those of us who work at SLACs seemingly insist on our own powerlessness?

Two answers occur to us. In the first place, those of us at SLACs accept systemic inertia because, by and large, it benefits us. Approximately 75 percent of the faculty at arts and sciences colleges that focus solely on undergraduate degrees are either tenured or on the tenure track. This is the reverse ratio of all other degree-granting institutions, where approximately 75 percent of the faculty are poorly paid contingent workers (Morphew et al. 13). In that context, while faculty and administrators at SLACs may grumble about salaries and benefits—and this is certainly *not* an argument for speeding up the signature neoliberal race to the bottom—in comparison with most employees in higher education, not to mention the "real" world, they do very well. According to the American Association of University Professors, the average salary for assistant professors at private baccalaureate colleges in 2019–20 was $77,463. Presidents averaged $428,337, and chief academic officers averaged about half that. Professional staff, on the other hand, fare much worse, as do service workers. Faculty and administrators, however, are generally paid well to do a job that also has great meaning for them; and most of them love it. It's hard to find a stronger reason for not wanting to rock the boat.

The second reason that explains why we sustain a system that eats at our souls rather than demanding action to change it, is that, to borrow from Marilynne Robinson, we have "surrendered thought to ideology" (2018 xii). The ideology in which we are embedded is that of *meritocracy*, the belief that education is the great equalizer, that those who climb its ladders most adroitly (including ourselves) are those who have done the best work, that the students who come our way all took off from the same starting line and are running the same race, and that we are engaged in the good fight to combat inequality (Markovits). Trained to be perpetually skeptical critics, we nonetheless ignore all the data that point in the exact opposite direction and that incriminate us for the role we play in sustaining inequality. We seek comfort and absolution in meritocracy's promise that those who succeed are the "best," even though, as Caitlin Zaloom of NYU has pointed out, this is nothing short of "absurd."

It is this same meritocratic model, manifested in the perception that some of our students come to us unprepared or underprepared, and therefore in need of "remediation," that leads many SLACs to immediately dismiss students who are thought to be in need of "fixing" because they don't conform to prevailing "humanist" (white or middle-class) identity. Our task, in the terms of this ideology, is to determine how to make "them" be more like "us," to shed notions of interdependence and community in favor of generating a strong, independent, individual voice. As Micere Keels observes, "Arguments for adopting a humanist identity are motivated by the assumption that Whites have shed their European identities ... [which] belies the fact that European customs and values permeate all aspects of American society, and therefore makes the humanist identity a colonized identity in which the price of inclusion is erasure through assimilation" (13). What colleges open with one hand, they close with the other by demanding cultural and epistemological conformity.

If this ideology operates in terms of the students SLACs are looking to admit, the same forces shape who those colleges hire, promote, and tenure. Faculty are granted entrance into a much desired protected space only after running the gauntlet of "demonstrating excellence" in the strangely trifurcated, and arbitrarily crafted, buckets of teaching, service, and research, knowing all the while that only publications that "accord with their senior colleagues' idea of what counts as scholarship" will actually matter (Menand). In handing over our power to an ideology of meritocracy and all that ideology implies, including its inherent racism, we have made ourselves into defenders of an educational caste system.

The dual crises brought on by a transitory pandemic and persistent, systemic racism are forcing us to confront two realities that we have heretofore avoided. First, if we are to survive, we must change our practices to take greater advantage of our unique characteristics as small liberal arts colleges. And second, if we are to be true to our values and aspirations, we can no longer ignore the ways we, within our own institutional cultures, reproduce the inequality and racism at the heart of the nation. As Claudia Rankine put it, we must "disorder the disorder."

In writing this manifesto, we are well-aware that we are not the first people to propose a glorious march into an uncertain future. We have participated in more than our fair share of strategic planning meetings over the years, gloomy affairs often marked by their (oddly combined and ever-present) strident pitch and ineffectiveness. If they tend to produce more cynicism than change, it is largely because they operate within the structures of powerlessness we have described, which can only generate a sense of hopelessness and inevitability. But, to borrow from Ibram X. Kendi, what gives us hope is "a simple truism. Once we give up hope, we are guaranteed to lose" (238). What *we* hope is that those of us in the liberal arts community will seize this do-or-die moment and take back the power we've all collectively surrendered. What *we* hope is that those who are not yet a part of a community at a small liberal arts college—students, parents, faculty, and administrators— will be so motivated by its radical reimagination that they will want to become a part of it too.

The good news is that the path forward, as we see it, is inherent in the very roots of the liberal arts. Discarding its partisan, blue state overtones, to be "liberal" is to be open to new ideas, behaviors, and opinions. It implies a willingness to discard traditions that impede needed change. As it relates to higher education, the term suggests a commitment to the broadening of general knowledge and experience, rather than training that is directed exclusively for a technical or professional field. To be immersed in the "arts" is to commit to the open expression and application of creative skills, to the powerful unleashing of the human imagination in all fields of endeavor. Taken together, these terms emphasize openness, innovation, creativity, and the extension of knowledge. They describe an orientation to the world that is expansive, dynamic, and productive. The culture we envision intentionally cultivates this orientation in all of its members and enacts these virtues in every facet of the community. It embodies our pivotal understanding that higher education is a public good and, as such, must be readily accessible, welcoming, and open to everyone; that, as process and not product, it must teach, practice, and enhance democracy; and, finally, that it can and should foster social mobility and social justice through inclusive, culturally sustaining, and anti-racist practices. Together, this culture will help define how small liberal arts colleges think about the purpose of an education, plan their curriculum, and design their frameworks of teaching and learning.

Culture: Defining Our Terms

"Culture eats strategy for breakfast," the management consultant Peter Drucker once observed. And while we would endorse *anything* that would consume the strategic planning processes that have devoured countless hours of our careers, it has become clear to us that institutional change will only come about when institutional culture changes. That is as true for SLACs as it is for any other organization. We require a culture that can support and sustain the changes needed to resuscitate, revitalize, and reclaim the small liberal arts college; a culture that is goal-oriented, inclusive, flexible, innovative, collaborative, and supportive; a culture where individuals take their power seriously and are accountable for the results they produce.

In trying to imagine a holistic way of conceiving of education in these relatively idiosyncratic places we call home, we realize we need to begin by laying out the features and characteristics that foreground the culture to which we aspire—a culture that provides a space for SLACs to reclaim their power and that categorically rejects meritocratic and assimilationist approaches. There are many glimmers of this new culture already operative at different colleges, and we take inspiration from them, but what we envision doesn't yet fully exist. Among its prominent aspects are the following:

1) It Is Authentically Motivated: The promise of a "meritocratic ideal," as Daniel Markovits has pointed out, the notion that "social and economic rewards should track achievement rather than breeding," is no longer operative, if it ever has been. Deference to the external goals and metrics determined by *U.S. News*-style ranking systems has blocked students from lower- and middle-income families from competing on a level playing field while simultaneously saddling *all* students with the anxieties inherent in a process that guarantees, by the system's own measures, that almost everyone will fail. A meritocracy embedded in neoliberal values has "banishe[d] the majority of citizens to the margins of their own society" (xiv). The opposite of a "meritocratic idea" is not the lack of standards or the absence of rewards for sustained work; it is a culture galvanized by authentic motivation, whether on the part of an individual, a group, a community, or an institution. The culture, inspired by authentic, multidimensional goals, values effort, welcomes collaboration, and insists on democratic inclusion.

2) It Is Culturally Sustaining and Nonassimilationist: The dominant ideology in higher education determines that students should bring their "academic" selves to college, leaving behind any attachments they have to their social identities and their uniqueness (Keels 13). For white students, becoming their "academic" selves has meant they have had to jump through a series of hoops designed by a standardized testing regime that has pushed them to be like everyone else. For students of color, entrance into historically white colleges has also meant assimilation into a white, middle-class culture, a process of racist transformation that begins long before their first day of classes. As Zora Neale Hurston wrote of her experience in 1928 as the only Black student at Barnard, "Among the thousand white persons, I am a dark rock surged upon, and overswept" (3). The new culture we're advocating for rejects assimilation in favor of meeting people where they are, and then building value from each individual's lived experience. We'd like to see this basic principle applied in every facet of the way people interact in this community— from the classroom to the nurturing of authentic teaching and administrative practices. We want to see a culture that pushes back against norming and conforming in every regard. The nonassimilationist culture we require at SLACs will support the transformative impact of education even as it allows students to sustain their social identities and draw strength from their lived experience. "Through it all, I remain myself," Hurston concluded, "When covered by the waters, I am; and the ebb but reveals me again" (3).

3) It Is Inclusive and Antiracist: While it should be clear from the above, SLACs must foster a culture that is not just "inclusive" in a quantitative sense—adding to the number of "diverse" faces and experiences on campus—but that is also actively antiracist. It must generate a culture that is aware of the way that anti-Black racism, in particular, is a systemic part of our institutions and must be addressed and resisted. This culture must encourage bold, creative approaches that promise to move us more rapidly toward justice and that will require relinquishing or sharing power in ways that may make people who currently hold power uncomfortable, which is as it should be.

4) It Is Integrative: The small liberal arts college must cultivate a culture that values integration at all levels—within the curriculum, between the curriculum and the co-curriculum, and between the college and the community. The culture we seek doesn't have silos, invisible walls, compartments, or departments. No one wants to live in a box, and we don't want them to. We want a culture where people can bring their whole selves in, one that doesn't ask them to divide what they "know" from what they care about or who they are, to carve up knowledge into fragments, or to tear themselves into pieces.

5) It Uses Backwards-Design Thinking: The principle of backwards design is essentially product- and outcome-oriented. It rests on the premise that when you start with a goal in mind, the steps you take to get there generally end up being more intentional, productive, unscripted, and uncharted than they would be without that vision. Backwards design is the space of innovation, a process that nurtures creative problem-solving and opens up possibility.

6) It Emphasizes Collaborative Autonomy: Somewhat of a contradiction in terms, collaborative autonomy suggests a culture that trusts, values, and empowers individuals to control the shape of their experience while, at the same time, flourishing from the energy that results from collaboration and bringing a shared vision to life. We want a community of innovative and interdependent thinkers—people who see things differently and who crave being around others who see things differently, people who push others to challenge their own perceptions and perspectives, and people who put their different ways of seeing into action for the good of the community. We want rogue thinkers who value collaboration and enact solidarity.

7) It Is a Space of Productive Restlessness: Isabelle Roche, of Bennington College, used this term to describe the "curiosity that drives [the faculty's] professional work, teaching, and mentorship." We love it. It captures perfectly the kind of orientation we're hoping each and every person will bring to this reimagined community. Productive restlessness is fueled by outward-looking, big-picture, high-stakes thinking. The "productively restless" are those who are internally driven to put things out into the world, to make things happen. They are individuals, and by extension communities, who feel a great sense of urgency to make the world a better place and who won't be bound by a need to conform to arbitrary external expectations.

8) It Fosters Accountability: People who manifest productive restlessness generally also know better than anyone else when and where they are falling short. We want to create a culture where people are accountable to their own high expectations and where, in the midst of these high expectations, we can help one another, in formative ways, to be our best selves and do our best work. The kind of culture we seek is not punitive, suspicious, distrustful, or intent on calling people out for bad behavior. It starts with the optimistic sense that people *do* want to be their best selves, that the antagonisms that crop up in a community can be dismantled when we understand their origins. We want to see a culture that actively works to address those antagonisms, which paradoxically means sometimes making them visible so that they don't fester. We want to create a culture where we collectively agree that we won't tolerate certain ways of treating one another, and where we assume the responsibility of resisting practices that damage the community.

———

We begin with three global recommendations. Our first is inspired by the student author of that prophetic thesis from part 1, who wished that their college experience had been characterized by a "full on commitment to the mission." Mission-speak is all the rage these days. By invoking it, we don't mean to empty it of meaning. What we mean, and what we think this student meant, is that whatever a college's mission is (and we are in no way advocating for all SLACs to adopt the same mission), *every one* of the institution's decisions should be made in the service of that mission. These decisions should be characterized by intentionality, they should practice inclusive deliberation and transparency, and they should demonstrate commitment. We don't think this is currently happening at most small liberal arts colleges.

Our second recommendation comes from an understanding born of experience that the only way to make the kind of changes we're advocating for is if SLACs forge a culture of internal solidarity. Rather than an empty, "we're all in this together" gesture, when we know "we're" not, authentic solidarity demands a new mode of decision-making, one that foregrounds the college's mission and speaks for the entire institution that supports that mission.

Finally, we understand that we can't do this alone. Our third recommendation is that SLACs must collaborate with each other, because only in unity is there the strength we require. Breaking from the false meritocracy that is represented by *U.S. News* requires unity in action. It is an action that can help save our colleges, both economically and morally. Catharine Hill, former president of Vassar, recently warned of the financial risks when colleges try to "out-prestige" each other (Blumenstyk). And Fumio Sugihara, dean of admissions and financial aid at Hampshire College, pointed to the fact that Hampshire "chose our mission and values over rankings" when it made the decision not to accept SAT/ACT test scores for admissions (Jaschik 2020). Neither *U.S. News* nor the testing companies, which are part of a billion-dollar business, will give up easily, and *U.S. News & World Report* has already announced that it will begin to rank "test-blind" colleges. But it's long past time that we let the tail wag the dog, and collaboration among SLACs will be essential to achieving that goal.

We are not offering a roadmap, a detailed "how-to" guide for creating this culture at the post-pandemic liberal arts college. To do so would give the false impression that one can "arrive" at the "ideal" liberal arts college. Instead, the college we seek to create is always in process, never a completed product. It is always growing, never fully grown. And to sustain it, we turn our attention to three areas:

> 1) *People*, particularly the processes whereby SLACs admit students, hire faculty, and appoint administrators.

> 2) *Institution*, including the forms of internal organization that support and extend the college's mission; and

> 3) *Classroom Culture and the Learning Environment*, which explores the requirements of transformative, inclusive, and student-centered learning.

Finally, we address a number of financial approaches, and the public support many require, that can guide SLACs toward a more sustainable future, even—especially—as they adopt need-blind admissions policies.

PEOPLE

The most important factor in shaping the new culture we crave is, obviously, the people who create it.

Getting people onto our campuses who are eager to plunge into this vibrant, productive, diverse, welcoming, and collaborative space is more than half the battle. Asserting our ability to determine who populates our campuses is the initial, and probably the most fundamental, step in reclaiming the power we have to radically reimagine our colleges in ways that serve students, parents, faculty, and administrators alike. By rejecting the false meritocracy generated under neoliberalism, we are likewise rejecting practices that have perpetuated elitism and racism, closed off opportunities, and erected a nearly impregnable caste system. Using their *own* criteria, SLACs will select students, faculty, and administrators who share in the culture of productive restlessness colleges should seek to promote. Through this process, they can revive the promise of the small liberal arts college to be a true engine of equity and inclusion, an institution that supports deep learning, broad connection, and social mobility.

Admissions: Students

We begin with admissions. It is perhaps the most important decision that SLACs make, particularly because all liberal arts colleges use selective, rather than open, admissions practices. If we are sincere about wanting to shift to a more collaborative, equitable, and energizing culture in our colleges, the admissions office is where we have to start.

Our current admissions process is marked both by moral failure and logical perversity. By essentially allowing *U.S. News & World Report* and the other rating systems to guide and shape the admissions process, we have chosen to let others make our most important decisions for us. SLACs have become complicit in an elitist system that has long hidden under the guise of a competitive meritocracy. An admissions process, for example, that expends resources to attract more and more applicants just so more and more of them can be rejected lays bare the condition of false choice many SLACs have collectively contrived for their students.

From the moment students enter kindergarten, they are told what it means to "succeed." They are funneled into paths and tracks they very well might not have chosen for themselves, while simultaneously being presented with conflicting messages. Some, those who are on the "college track," are reassured that they are the best and the brightest and can do anything they choose. But they are also told what to learn, how to learn it, and how to demonstrate that they have learned. Other students, those on the "vocational track," get a more pointed message: You'll never succeed, so you might as well give up.

By the time the students in the first category apply for college, they face the truly Kafkaesque task of writing an application essay in which they must show simultaneously what makes them unique from thousands of other applicants, *and* how they have taken the same classes and participated in the same extracurricular activities that everyone else has. Writing in the *New York Times*, Jeffrey Selingo recently advised students, who were thinking about whether to craft their application essays around "their coronavirus experiences," to consider, "how much Covid-19 is too much?" After instructing applicants to "bring to the essay the same level of details and specifics that admissions officers expect when applicants write about anything that has shaped their life," the article closes with a reminder to fretful writers: "And remember, the essay is very rarely the thing that helps get an applicant in anyway." Prompts like these only recapitulate the "tell-us-what-you-think-we-want-to-hear" guessing game of high-stakes testing, which ultimately breeds resentment and cynicism. It is one more way we ask students to become "unique individuals" while we simultaneously require that they look like everybody else who's headed in the same direction.

It's no wonder that the culture of testing, deployed as a sorting mechanism and rationalized as an absolute prerequisite for admission to elite colleges, has been part of a process that has torqued student apprehension and depression to historic levels, fueled admissions scandals, and deepened the inequalities of an already elitist system. A recent report by a consortium of teacher educators and led by the Harvard Graduate School of Education, lamented the competitive frenzy surrounding college admissions and warned that it posed a direct threat to applicants' mental health. Harvard should know. In 2020, they admitted 1,980 students and rejected 38,268 others. This is a system that renders students sick, angry, invisible, and effectively powerless.

At the same time, the hyper-competitive admissions process has become an economy that has potentially turned liberal arts colleges into generic, faceless institutions, their unique characteristics, histories, missions, and values flattened out into a transactional exchange that gets performed through the whirlwind college tour. After twelve college visits, applicants and their families generally come away with bits of trivia (why the halls are so wide; which gate not to walk through if you want to graduate on time), a hazy memory of a tour guide who seemed cool, and perhaps a visit to an interesting class. We exist in an economy that has taken the choice out of college attendance—you must get a degree in order to get ahead—and, at the same time, has celebrated exclusivity and consecrated scarcity. This means students who don't actually want to attend your college but feel they *have* to, are likely taking seats away from those who wish they could be there with every fiber of their being.

It seems counterintuitive to cite one of the nation's most competitive activities—the Scripps National Spelling Bee—as a model that illustrates the approach we desire for SLAC admissions, but it suggests a combination of individual passion, hard work, and commitment that actually could make for a healthier admissions process. When the coronavirus pandemic canceled the 2020 Bee, one of the contestants, Vayun Krishna, an eighth grader from Sunnyvale, California, was asked whether he would miss being with the community of spellers the competition creates. Krishna responded, "You're not really competing against the spellers themselves, you're competing against the dictionary . . . the only thing you can control is what *you* do." In the end, he concluded, "you meet a lot of people who have the same passion as you, which is a passion for words and language. It's pretty easy to make friends with them" (Martin). The admissions process we propose is one in which students can identify *their* passions, rather than having those passions defined by a rankings-oriented admissions system. It is a place where students welcome the possibility of engaging with others in community because they don't have to view college as a zero-sum game in which their win entails someone else's loss.

It will be difficult to push back against such a deeply entrenched system. We know that, and our recommendations for how to change the process reflect both optimism and realism. The new process we have in mind would reject the metrics of "most likely to succeed" to which students have been subjected for so long, criteria that feed into a process known as undermatching, where low-income students and many students of color are discouraged from even applying to selective colleges (Harris). Instead, it would center on students' individual stories, hopes, and dreams, and it would highlight the unique features and benefits of SLACs themselves. It would be a process, in other words, that replaces false choice with *actual* choice for everyone involved.

The process we have in mind requires four interrelated changes: 1) the adoption of need-blind admissions; 2) a change to admissions criteria; 3) a revision of the recruitment process; and 4) a revamping of the application process.

1) Adopting Need-Blind Admissions: Andrew Delbanco begins his engaging *College: What It Was, Is, and Should Be* by recounting how, as a young faculty member at Columbia, he voted to retain the university's "need-blind" admissions system without actually understanding what he was voting for (xii). Columbia's faculty chose to retain the system. I (Steve) sat through a similar vote at Oberlin some years ago. The faculty voted to replace "need-blind" with "need-aware" admissions. Like Delbanco, I was largely unaware of what the issue was about and was swayed by the argument that Oberlin couldn't always afford to admit students without regard to the applicant's financial need. Sometimes the college needed to consider who could pay, particularly when all the other application characteristics were the same. Years later, as liberal arts colleges have become preserves of the wealthy, I will admit that I made a mistake. It's not that the financial calculations were off; just that we put those calculations ahead of Oberlin's social responsibility, ahead of the college's mission. Now, facing the crisis of their lifetimes, SLACs must start with the basic realization that they will never become truly diverse and equitable colleges unless they admit students without considering financial need. We will address the financial measures that can help us achieve this goal in the "Finances" section below. But, put simply, if SLACs don't change this one feature, they will continue to admit a much larger portion of their students from the top 20 percent of the income distribution than from the bottom 80 percent. They will continue to be engines of inequality.

2) Changing Admissions Criteria: SLACs must sever ties with the "ranking and rating" systems, captained by *U.S. News & World Report*, and reassert their power to determine their own criteria for admitting the students *they* want at their colleges. Considering other elements of the false meritocracy,

SLACs also need to terminate their reliance on standardized testing (the SAT and ACT), reevaluate the weight given to GPA or class ranking, and reconsider the bonuses given to students who bring in an armload of AP courses (particularly since colleges are discounting the credits earned in such courses). An abundance of research points to the way that testing and standard measures of K-12 achievement such as the GPA reflect racial and class discrimination (Dixon-Roman et al., Gregory et al.). To use those same measures as a primary basis of admissions decisions, logically, only validates and reproduces that discrimination. The decision to admit a student at a "selective" college is grounded in a calculation of who is "most likely to succeed" which is largely based on these traditional metrics. What we are suggesting is an admissions process that asks "who is most likely to succeed" based on other indicators, indicators that take account of determination and resilience, of who can succeed when placed in an environment where faculty, staff, and peers are knitted together to provide the level of support which each student requires.

SLACs, like other selective colleges, should also end the practice of legacy admissions. A century-old process that gives preference to the children of alumni, legacy admissions share a repugnant history with older patterns of discrimination against Black and Jewish people. As Evan Mandery, Harvard class of 1989, argued, "There's no plausible moral claim that accidents of birth that advantage you—like being a man, or being a white man, or being a rich, white man—should give you a further advantage" (Larkin and Aina). And though the discussion of affirmative action is a broader one than we can engage with here, we would note, as Zeus Leonardo put it, that white people have reaped its benefits for 360 years and continue to do so under contemporary conditions of systemic racism.

3) Revising Recruitment: SLACs need to recognize and challenge the assimilationist assumptions that—even though hidden behind a call for more "diversity"—actually obscure the fact that most colleges continue to look for, and find, students who are culturally and socially homogenous; that is, white and middle-class. SLACs, like other colleges and universities, display their priorities by virtue of where they send admissions staff to recruit students. These visits have an outsized influence on where students—particularly first-generation students—apply and enroll. It is disturbing, then, as studies have shown, that colleges use their admissions resources to recruit at whiter, wealthier high schools (Jaquette and Salazar). At the same time, research (and common sense) indicates that students from less affluent backgrounds are more likely to apply (and attend) if they are recruited and "feel wanted" (Holland). SLACs should extend their recruitment visits to include more diverse schools, both in terms of income and race. They should also craft admissions materials that foreground factors that are more likely to yield a diverse class of students who are eager to embrace the challenges and opportunities of participating in the kind of learning community SLACs are trying to establish—with the clear understanding that the colleges are committed to creating the welcoming environment they advertise.

4) Revamping the Admissions Process: Finally, we advocate for substituting the standard application essay with organic, face-to-face conversations that would identify students who are actively choosing the SLAC model for themselves and would provide plenty of room for students to express their visions for the paths they want to pursue. To implement this, we would supplement admissions staff with additional students and further mobilize alumni, staff, and faculty who are eager to reach out to, and welcome, the kind of students the college actually wants.

Hiring Practices
It is crucial that SLACs change their admissions process. But we also argue for a radical shift in hiring practices in order to recruit faculty, staff, and administrators who can bring this new culture to life. As a general framework, we find it helpful to borrow from the world of social entrepreneurism, calling for practices that will identify community-driven risk-takers, individuals who exemplify the productive restlessness we want to instill in the culture. It's Carol Dweck's "growth mindset" we're after, and that mindset should be built into every facet of an institution. Dweck describes the link between individual and institution like this:

> Individuals who believe their talents can be developed (through hard work, good strategies, and input from others) have a growth mindset. They tend to achieve more than those with a more fixed mindset (those who believe their talents are innate gifts). This is because they worry less about looking smart and they put more energy into learning. When entire companies embrace a growth mindset, their employees report feeling far more empowered and committed; they also receive far greater organizational support for collaboration and innovation (Harvard Business).

The hiring practices we envision, like the new admissions process, push back against the false meritocratic and damaging assimilationist thinking that contribute to the fixed mindset and psychology of scarcity that currently define SLACs. A growth mindset corrects the notion that students and faculty (or *every* member of the community, for that matter) arrive with a fixed set of talents and/or traits—that people either demonstrate "brilliance" and "excellence" when they arrive on campus, or they don't. The paradigm shift we're calling for is one that expects and nurtures growth and, in that way, breathes life, energy, excitement, and innovation into the community. When it comes to combating chain-sickness, SLACs should think about how to nurture job satisfaction and how to bring people into the room who are committed and enthusiastic about cocreating the institution's visions.

Faculty

Currently, faculty hiring at most liberal arts colleges is closely tied to graduate school priorities, organization, and prestige. For decades, hiring has taken place in a buyers' market; colleges search an overabundance of applicants to hire the candidate who best matches their needs and interests. Typically, tenure track openings at liberal arts colleges draw hundreds of eager, if not desperate, applicants. In history, for example, 1,003 doctorates were awarded in 2018, but only 319 jobs were advertised for tenure track assistant professorships that same year. Many of those who did not get hired that year, of course, joined the myriad job seekers on the market the following year. And yet, with a perpetually wide and broad field of possible candidates— why graduate schools continue to overproduce doctoral candidates is another question altogether—evidence indicates that the single most important factor in determining who will be hired is the prestige of their doctoral program. A study of nearly 19,000 tenure track or tenured faculty revealed that almost 90 percent of all hires, depending on their field, came from a quarter of all doctoral-granting institutions (Clauset et al.).

Frankly, we have trouble understanding the narrow attraction that these prestigious institutions hold on hiring committees. Once again, SLACs have handed over their power to others when deciding who they want as faculty. In this case, power has been portioned out to high-ranking graduate programs, programs that don't necessarily appreciate what we do at liberal arts colleges. Anecdotes run rampant at SLACs of faculty members who were actively dissuaded by their graduate school advisors from pursuing a position at a liberal arts college, the implication being that it would be a sign of failure to end up at an institution that prioritizes undergraduate teaching. This is not surprising; pedagogy tends to be treated as an afterthought in the graduate programs many of us hail from. It is also the case that most of these programs continue to privilege traditional fields, which are sliced into ever more specialized subjects of study.

Likewise, academic publishing is still seen as the *sine qua non* of accomplishment, despite the obscurity of many of the subjects and the miniscule audiences they attract. Outsiders poke fun at the seemingly impenetrable prose used in academic papers, but often we as academics struggle to comprehend what we are reading in our own fields. These practices are surprisingly at odds with SLACs' oft-repeated values of broad-based knowledge, interdisciplinarity, and the cultivation of writing, research, and pedagogy that can speak to a wider audience and cultivate an intelligent citizenry. A colleague once remarked that she wanted her biology students to be able to give oral presentations "so that even a governor could understand them," yet SLACs don't seem to hire faculty with these same criteria in mind. Instead, they continue to reproduce practices that undermine their mission, often missing out on candidates who would be much better fits for their campuses but who haven't passed through prestigious programs. In hiring, SLACs need to be less subservient to the prestige economy and more attentive to those faculty who can best serve the colleges' new mission.

So what kind of faculty do we, should we, want to join SLACs? Here's an imagined job posting to describe our vision:

> We seek teacher-practitioners who value collaboration and co-creation (between themselves and students, colleagues, staff, and administration); are eager to promote integration across the curriculum, between the classroom and the co-curriculum, and between the campus and the broader community; and who would willingly contribute to an institutional culture of inclusion. The faculty we seek to recruit are risk-takers, agents of change, and producers of new knowledge with demonstrated success in the application of their fields. They will view students as collaborative partners and co-creators, individuals with their own powerful lived experiences who have the capacity to shape their own learning.

At the present time, if candidates are more than five years out from having received their doctorate, their chances of getting hired at one of our institutions is, almost literally, nil. And yet SLACs need to be positively disposed to hiring faculty who possess experience in and beyond academia, who can serve the students' interests, and who come to the college via less traditional paths.

It is also important for SLACs to establish a symmetry between the faculty they recruit and the students they're hoping to attract through the new admissions process. Both groups of people should be risk-takers, agents of change, and producers of new knowledge. This will help combat the hypocrisy-cynicism complex by building a learning community with a shared work ethic as its primary feature.

Much like the conversational approach we propose for reshaping admissions, the mechanism we envision for faculty recruitment would similarly invite candidates into open and transparent conversations about how their skill sets and experiences resonate with the mission of the college and stand to facilitate the fulfillment of that mission. Evidence, drawn from syllabi, assignments, letters from students and collaborators, projects, and other similar artifacts, would further inform this process, as would more authentic classroom presentations than is currently the norm.

In this current moment of crisis, we cannot remain unaware of, or unconcerned with, the ways that higher education, including our own SLACs, has abjectly failed to create a truly diverse faculty. Of all full-time faculty in postsecondary institutions in 2017, only 3 percent were Black or Latinx (National Center). We should not be surprised, then, that a 2019 Gallup survey revealed that only a fifth of Black graduates felt their professors "cared about them as a person" (Harlan and Marken). But this issue is not just a question of numbers, and the responsibility for caring about Black students should not add to the emotional labor, the "racial battle fatigue," already carried by faculty of color (Hartlep and Ball). Far too few institutions have actually shown themselves to be welcoming of a diversity of approaches, cultures, epistemologies, or types of community that these hires offer, something that is felt deeply by faculty of color (Laymon). "Even though we black scholars and students, in most cases, have worked hard and overcome significant impediments to get here," Stefan M. Bradley, the chair of Loyola Marymount's African American studies department, recently wrote, "maintaining a modicum of dignity means realizing that we may never be fully included at our colleges. . . . I have . . . witnessed other black professionals lose parts of their souls to fulfill the compromise." The hiring practices we propose for the reimagined SLAC must be anti-assimilationist and antiracist by nature. SLACs must actively demonstrate their commitment to equality by challenging their own structures and taking the necessary risks to become antiracist institutions that practice, on an ongoing basis, an openness to self-critique and change.

Implications for the Faculty Career

How would this new hiring criteria align with the current (and rapidly disappearing) tenure system? Tenure has traditionally offered vital protections to academic freedom. As the American Association of University Professors notes, "When faculty members can lose their positions because of their speech, publications, or research findings, they cannot properly fulfill their core responsibilities to advance and transmit knowledge." Similarly, tenure protections act to slow, if not stop, administrators' desire to reduce labor costs by replacing full-time senior faculty (and their higher salaries), with beginning or contingent faculty, an issue of no small concern in a labor market with an overabundance of PhDs and at the moment of the COVID-19 crisis.

But serious questions have been raised about both the efficacy and the ethics of the tenure system. In past times of crisis, such as the McCarthy era, tenured and untenured faculty were actually fired at the same rate (Lewis). In more recent cases where legislatures and trustees have pressured colleges to dismiss faculty for statements they have made or written, the more principled administrators have stood by their faculty regardless of whether they were tenured or not, stressing the principle of academic freedom, not the privilege of tenure. And tenured faculty have been distressingly late to the game in terms of advocating for the rights of contingent faculty and instructors (Hacker and Dreifus 142–43).

At the same time, the tenure system, with its make-or-break decision after six or seven probationary years, can distort careers and the nature of a faculty member's productive engagement on both sides of the tenure decision. It can also lessen accountability (and sometimes collegiality) from those who have made it past the barrier, which tends to hand excessive power to senior (usually white) faculty and administrators. As Louis Menand has wryly observed, assistant professors "are free to write what they choose, [but] what they write had better accord with their senior colleagues' idea of what counts as scholarship."

The impact of the current tenure system on faculty of color is beyond troubling. According to 2017 data, Black faculty make up 5.2 percent of all tenured faculty at baccalaureate institutions, while whites make up almost 80 percent (Heilig et al.). The causes behind such disparities were made painfully clear by Marlene L. Daut, a professor of African American Studies at the University of Virginia, who wrote in a 2019 essay in the *Chronicle of Higher Education* about how her "career was threatened—from the classroom to the conference room, and from the publishing house to the foundation world—by everyday racist and discriminatory behaviors for which there are still no mitigating policies."

We're not advocating for the removal of tenure or rank from current faculty. Any new system would need to protect those who entered into employment under a tenure system. But if SLACs are looking for faculty who are risk-takers, agents of change, and producers of new knowledge, if they are authentically committed to overturning structural racism, if they want to encourage faculty to set and achieve goals that they find meaningful and that are consistent with larger institutional goals, and if they want to grant *all* faculty the right to academic freedom, and not just the privileged few, then they might well want to move proactively to replace the current tenure system with one based on variable length and renewable contracts. And faculty should certainly move for this change before the decision is taken out of their hands with much less favorable results.

Any new system would have to provide the same strong protections for faculty rights that are currently enshrined in the tenure process, extending them to the instructional staff as a whole. A variable-length contract system, along the lines of that adopted by Bennington College, for example, would allow faculty to set individual goals that can change over time to better align with institutional priorities and an individual's own career and personal rhythms. This would create the conditions for periods of greater focus on pedagogy, research, administration, or community involvement. As opposed to a "make-or-break" system arriving in the seventh year, a variable-length contract system would open multiple points for professional development and formative intervention. Driven by an institutional commitment to equity and an understanding that knowledge is produced in multiple ways, this new system could more adequately protect vulnerable faculty—including those who teach in interdisciplinary fields, and faculty of color who, whether inside or outside a tenure system, face the (unacknowledged) emotional labor of advising and mentoring students of color while also serving as the "racial conscience" of their institutions—by reducing the traditionalists' grip on the curriculum, promoting new approaches, and ensuring a greater commitment to the "productive restlessness" we desire. We are also quite sure that if you build it, they will come. As the Bennington example has already demonstrated, this approach would attract faculty who are eager to make their careers in such an environment.

Administration

In writing this manifesto, it occurred to us that a key feature in the chain-sickness and hypocrisy-cynicism complex we've described, and a key way that SLACs enact their own powerlessness, is through a self-defeating practice of dismissing visionary leadership as a possibility that exists in the world. We're talking to you, faculty!

Faculty *know* visionary when they see it, they *know* what it feels like to be inspired and energized by someone who *gets* the liberal arts and who helps instructors clarify their promise and purpose. Faculty know this, but at the end of the day, most of them just don't want to be organized for change. Most of them got into this business precisely because they are self-driven. They crave the autonomy that comes with pursuing questions they find compelling, and they're inherently distrustful of people telling them what to do. In many ways, this cynicism is bred from the patterns faculty have seen played out too often on their campuses, by the ways that they have been bruised by college presidents who have *not* had the faculty's best interests at heart, who have looked at their presidency as a stepping stone to "bigger and better" institutions, spent lavishly and exorbitantly from our endowments to *build, build, build* on our campuses, and then moved on as others were left to deal with the damage. We get it. But here's the thing: if SLACs want to facilitate a cultural shift toward the kind of community we are envisioning here, faculty cannot continue to be agents of their own cynicism. Instead, they need to enthusiastically welcome recruiting a new kind of administrator—systems-thinkers, practitioners, and, yes, visionaries—who viscerally understand and reject meritocratic and assimilationist thinking, who value transparency and collaboration with all constituents, and who are able to communicate the institution's vision to faculty, staff, students, parents, alumni, trustees, and the broader community in ways that motivate and inspire everyone. And they're going to need to trust them to be leaders.

Again we look to social entrepreneurism and leaders who can, as one definition puts it, "pursue novel applications that have the potential to solve community-based problems . . . [and] are willing to take on the risk and effort to create positive changes in society through their initiatives." These are leaders who will pursue financial stability by enhancing the mission of their institution, who are committed to need-blind access and equity, and who don't view financial stability and intentional decisions to enhance community as mutually exclusive practices. Ideally, both administrators and faculty need to be held accountable to a shared vision and also have the capacity to hold others accountable when they act to undermine it. All this suggests that the knowledge, skills, and dispositions needed to lead such an institution can arise from many different fields. But a deep appreciation for the college community as a very specific form of intentional community must determine where SLACs search and how they select senior administrators. In proposing this new kind of community, we repeat the importance of solidarity as a cohesive force, which involves a new way of decision-making that foregrounds the college's mission and represents the entire institution that supports it.

We can be optimistic that the leadership SLACs require is already present on some campuses and that more leaders will soon follow. The presidents of Swarthmore, Pomona, and Oberlin, for example, have emphasized the important role liberal arts colleges play in times of national crisis with their responses to anti-Black racism and the police violence that exploded during the summer of 2020. Similarly, we can look optimistically to the statement of Lori White, who began her presidency at DePauw in July 2020 and who described her leadership approach in an email to the campus community as both "values-driven and inclusive . . . a collective process to which each of you has an opportunity to offer your voice." Her message was a welcome recognition that "part of our learning environment is to figure out together what it means to study, work, and live in a diverse, equitable and inclusive community." We are not surprised that all these presidents are African-American women who have felt the burden of anti-Blackness in their own lives.

Laura Walker, who was recently appointed as president at Bennington College, provides another example of the kind of leader we're advocating for. Her background is unusual for SLAC presidents in that she is not a "traditional" academic, but instead brings with her a wealth of experience and expertise in journalism, nonprofit management, and the arts. It's precisely this wider scope of experience, and the way Walker's background perfectly aligns with Bennington's values and goals, that we find to be a source of great opportunity. As staunch advocates of broadening what constitutes "expert knowledge" in the classroom and curriculum, we think it's critical for colleges to appoint presidents who have both charted innovative paths and who are avid champions for SLACs because they understand the relationship between the liberal arts approach and innovation.

Professional Staff

Who you gonna' call? When you need research help, when you are designing assignments, when your computer crashes, when you want to take your class to the museum. For these necessities, and many others, faculty turn to the professional staff for help. Yet the more that faculty depend on the support provided by librarians, IT personnel, curators, and technicians, the less *they* seem to be supported, or even noticed, by the faculty or the institution. Cuts to the professional staff were severe during the 2008 recession, and many have never been replaced, leaving fewer people to handle an ever-growing clamor for immediate attention. Adjusted for inflation, salaries for librarians/educational services providers at baccalaureate colleges in 2018-19 remain below what they were six years earlier. Salaries for IT personnel and lab technicians have crept up slightly over that same time, but all remain substantially below what beginning assistant professors on the tenure track are paid (Chronicle Data). As we recommend below, faculty at SLACs should be coordinating curriculum planning and course design to a much greater extent with librarians, IT personnel, and museum curators, as well as with staff in residential life and student support services. Each of these professionals will possess expertise that can lend itself to the development of a more holistic pedagogical approach; this will benefit the students while increasing a college's ability to form cohesive communities that respect and reward the contributions of all its members.

Both of us have worked extensively and closely with staff members in the development and implementation of our courses—collaborating with curators from our campus art museum, for instance, on lesson plans, with research librarians on the design of student research projects, and with the directors of various student life centers on campus on methods to engage students in class.

In that context, SLACs should look to hire professional staff—particularly those with faculty- and student-facing responsibilities—with precisely the same qualities we have recommended for faculty and administrators. SLACs should welcome individuals who are trained and confident in their own specialties, who think expansively about their jobs, who are eager to collaborate intensively with others in order to produce the best possible learning outcomes for the students, and who are eager to assume responsibility for the creation of a new community. Just as we recommend that professional staff play a role in the hiring of new faculty, so we suggest that faculty be consulted in the hiring of staff in those areas where there is likely to be significant interactions in the future.

INSTITUTION

By rejecting a false, meritocratic system and instead bringing to our campuses students, staff, faculty, and administrators who are deeply aligned with our missions, we have begun the process of reclaiming power from our self-imposed powerlessness. But what will we do with this power? Our argument is that SLACs must create institutions, and institutional cultures, that are better able to take advantage of what makes them unique in the universe of institutions of higher education: their relatively small number of students, highly residential nature, compact physical footprint, rich co-curricular offerings, and, in many cases, their close proximity to rural or exurban communities.

Let's put this in personal terms. The two of us work on campuses that enroll between 2,100 and 2,800 students. It takes us maybe twenty minutes to walk from one end of campus to the other, five minutes if we bike. Oberlin College and Conservatory has about 320 full-time faculty; DePauw, approximately 230. Compare this with Ohio State University, which sprawls over 16,000 acres and employs more than 7,000 faculty to teach 61,000 students.

Yet, remarkably similar to OSU, both Oberlin and DePauw are organized in ways that emphasize unit (or departmental) autonomy over institutional coherence. This organizational structure often overlooks opportunities for collaboration. It fosters scarcity-driven competition and makes it harder, rather than easier, for students to actively participate in planning their own programs of study, connect learning across classes and disciplines, or link their classroom experiences to residential life and the co-curriculum. We are quite sure that our two institutions are not outliers in this regard. This is not to say that students at Oberlin and DePauw don't derive important benefits that larger institutions can't offer. Rather, we are not using what we have to its full advantage. And if we are to emerge whole from the crisis brought on by the pandemic, that is what we must do.

In a culture of scarcity and suspicion, any recommendations for achieving a higher level of institutional integration will inevitably give rise to bloodletting concerns: whose ox will be gored this time? And in the context of the current pandemic, such exercises are bound to raise (justifiable) concerns that administrators will leverage the crisis to make changes they have long been eager to implement. It doesn't challenge the imagination in the slightest to observe that this not only will happen, but as we have already indicated, it is already happening. But if we are to change liberal arts colleges in essential ways, we need to build on a foundation of trust that is based on a shared vision and desired outcomes—something lacking in the broader society but still possible within our small communities. This is not, to be clear, a "just-trust-me" kind of trust; it is a trust that can only arise from extensive conversations that are anchored in transparency and grounded in participants' willingness to check their egos at the door.

At the institutional level, we offer two broad recommendations for this reimagined liberal arts college. First, SLACs should promote institutional integration, enhance learning opportunities across domains, and remove any and all barriers that inhibit or discourage collaboration. Second, these colleges should increase students' ability to plan their own course of study, take responsibility for their own learning, and become the creative and constructive members of the community that each one of them is supremely capable of being.

We recognize that there is no single model of academic organization that makes sense for every SLAC. Colleges that have operated for generations with departments at the heart of their academic and curricular organization will not easily adopt a "faculty-of-the-whole" approach to decision-making. There is no one-size-fits-all solution. That said, and based on our experiences teaching at two colleges with very strong departmental cultures, we have little doubt that a culture of strong, autonomous departments has ultimately prioritized local interests over institutional needs, which has made it harder to achieve important levels of cross-campus integration and collaboration. We need to consider what we are losing by preserving the current model of independent silos.

A system that encourages departments to request additional faculty positions or replacements, and where final decisions are made by a committee, dean, or provost, authorizes departments to consider only their own needs or desires, rather than focusing on broader institutional needs. Such an approach serves to stoke anger and suspicions about other departments—and the administration—when those requests are denied (as most will be). Such a practice is the scarcity-model equivalent of an admissions system that encourages more and more students to apply only to deny them entry. Models that instead encourage institutional thinking may not relieve the pain when a department doesn't get its replacement in Renaissance literature, but it will encourage academic units to more seriously consider the needs of the college as a whole.

A system that distributes resources based on the number of majors departments can attract likewise induces a competition for students, a practice which is both patronizing (we've all been to the lunches designed to capture prospective majors) and reinforces their status as consumers in an educational cafeteria. When a new student arrives on campus, the first question we ask them should not be, "What do you intend to major in?" but, "What do you want to get out of your education?" At Ursinus College, for example, students focus on four questions they are asked throughout their time on campus: What should matter to me? How should we live together? How can we understand the world? And what will I do? Bennington's model similarly directs students "toward self-fulfillment and ... constructive social purposes," placing the demanding work of formulating a program of study, scaffolded by good advising and peer support, on the students themselves, rather than by tempting them to grab a preassembled model, i.e., the "major." We support these kinds of approaches. A system that directs students to take responsibility for their own learning by designing individual programs of study is a powerful way to help them take ownership over their own learning, and it is central to the call for student empowerment, which we discuss in the next section.

A system that clusters all historians on one floor, philosophers on another, and chemists in a different building altogether, likewise prevents the kind of intellectual cross-fertilization that is ideal on a small campus. Examples abound of the ways that new insights can be reached through lateral learning, including MIT's famous Building 20, a temporary structure hurriedly constructed in 1943 that brought together, among many others, the likes of Amar Bose (acoustics), Harold Edgerton (photography), Jim Williams (analog circuits), and Noam Chomsky (linguistics). The counterarguments, of which we have heard many—How would we assign administrative assistants? Where would we get our mail?— only seem to further the case for moving faculty out of their current disciplinary stables into new ones that would open the possibility for wider intellectual exchange.

A system that reinforces a disciplinary focus, which is rooted in nineteenth-century epistemology, has produced greater and greater degrees of specialization while repressing, both among faculty and students, a move to the kind of interaction and integration that should be the calling card of small liberal arts institutions. We're not talking about the proliferation of interdisciplinary programs (Environmental Studies, Gender Studies, Latin American Studies, etc.) that link separate departments in the service of student majors. More often than not, the departments that cooperate in these majors remain autonomous and disinclined to explore larger convergences. (Further, faculty who are hired into interdisciplinary programs are required to respond to the demands that two or more departments place on them.) In fact, SLACs are capable of achieving an *integration of knowledge and meaning* that operates at a more profound level. Some have called for a move to a "third culture," beyond C. P. Snow's 1959 "two cultures" division between the sciences and the humanities, which would join, for example, science and art (Miller). While some of these steps are already underway at larger universities (the media labs at MIT and NYU, for example), we have only seen flashes of this at our own institutions when, for example, a biologist moves his office to the art department, or when students in a physics class curate an exhibit of William Eggleston's photography at the art museum.

Much more importantly, though, SLACs need to consider what they could gain by moving to a new organizational model. To the extent that the future of small liberal arts colleges will depend on their capacity to integrate and collaborate across campus, we need to transition from a culture that is invested in departmental autonomy into a culture that is capable of unifying the institution. As indicated above, there are a number of models colleges can explore. In some, the faculty operate as a "committee of the whole," without departments, where specific committees foreground institutional priorities in matters of personnel, curriculum design, or resource allocation. Other models cluster departments into traditional divisions (humanities, social sciences, science and math), where departments remain as a unit, but institutionally significant decisions such as hiring are recommended at the divisional level. Hiram College, for example, recently moved to organize academics around five interdisciplinary "schools" (science and sustainability, health and community advocacy, business and information analysis, education and civic leadership, and exploratory thought, creative arts, and languages). Still others are beginning to foster integration at a more functional, problem-solving level. We can already see this in the cognitive sciences, where faculty from biology, neuroscience, statistics, computer science, and psychology are beginning to cohere in a variety of planning capacities. If such root-and-branch reorganizations are too difficult, what can begin more quickly is a move to physically distribute faculty around the campus, a new emphasis on student-designed programs of study over departmental majors, and a removal of any silo-building practices that foster competition over collaboration.

Facilitating Connections between the Curriculum and the Co-curriculum

SLACs are "high-touch" institutions that allow for multiple points of contact between students and different parts of the campus. Typically, the responsibility for making those connections is left to the students themselves, and in many senses it should be. But colleges could do much more to support connections and promote integration between these parts. Consider the ways that current staff, who operate in separate silos but all support student learning (from the library to athletics, from residential life to student support services), could become an integral part of curricular and educational design discussions that currently take place within departments and exclusively among the faculty. In our experience, staff from these areas are invited to present at one department meeting during the year, if at all, and then they are often forgotten. In contrast to this type of model, academic planning that unites the classroom with the co-curriculum should be a regular and ongoing part of how we build a culture that supports student learning and responsibility.

One of the most successful methods we have seen for integrating the curriculum and co-curriculum is a faculty- and peer-supported e-portfolio system. E-portfolios are often used as virtual "lockers," where students store work from their classes and other activities. But they are most effective when they are used to promote self-directed learning and encourage students' deeper reflection on what they are learning. Studies have demonstrated that e-portfolios bolster a students' ability to self-assess performance, formulate learning goals, and determine future tasks. The e-portfolio system in place at LaGuardia Community College, for example, is designed to help students "document, deepen, and reflect on their learning experiences . . . connect their past and their future . . . their learning and their lives." By encouraging students to reflect on the full extension of their classroom, work, and social activities, e-portfolios can encourage students to connect classroom and co-curricular learning. A student who writes separate posts on her psychology class, her performance in a recent soccer match, and her interactions with cafeteria staff with whom she works in her campus dining hall job, can be prompted to think of the ways that insights drawn from one experience can be applied in other activities (Eynon and Gambino).

Reimagining Connections between "Student Life" and the Faculty

When Clark Kerr, the president of the University of California, introduced the concept of the "multiversity" in 1963, he stressed the emergence of an institution that, flush with federal research dollars, was "a prime instrument of national purpose" in which multiple constituencies—students, faculty, legislatures, governors—exerted pressure and vied for control. With the passage of federal legislation, particularly the Higher Education Act of 1965 and Title IX of the Education Amendments Act in 1972, colleges have become "multiversities" in more ways than Kerr envisioned.

Over the past few decades, colleges have been managing, supporting, and protecting students via a proliferation of "Student Life" offices. These offices provide professional mental health counseling. They advocate for students who have encountered sexual harassment, violence, racism, or other forms of discrimination. They coordinate disability accommodations and student academic support. They help international students. They offer career services, internships, and opportunities for community engagement. And they support the expression of students' spiritual lives. Many of these offices are absolutely essential, some are necessary, and a few of them seem to contribute only to the kind of administrative bloat imagined by Gregor Robinson's satirical website, universitytitlegenerator.com, where Kafkaesque titles are coupled with matching, outlandish salaries.

Robinson hoped that his humorous effort would "contribute to a broader discussion about where universities prioritize their resources, and help empower people to do something about the backwards state of affairs." We share Robinson's wish. For those who wonder about assistant and associate deans, who sometimes seem to sprout like mushrooms after a summer rain, the data confirm those suspicions. The swelling of administrative ranks over the past few decades has far outstripped faculty growth. Between 1987 and 2012, universities and colleges collectively added more than a half-million administrators and professional employees, outpacing both additions to the faculty and the rate of growth of the student body.

But our concerns are more qualitative than quantitative. As student life offices have multiplied, faculty have often stepped back from a prior expectation that they, too, are responsible for their students' lives. Instead, many faculty, whether it's due to their preferences, their increasing professional responsibilities, or external signals to "back off," have chosen to focus more exclusively on that smaller parcel of a student's life that unfolds on MWF between 9:00 and 9:50 a.m. in a physics or German class.

We're not arguing for the removal of student life professionals who have been hired over the past few years. Many of them are essential, and faculty are not trained in the fields in which these professionals engage. Rather, we're arguing for fuller faculty involvement with students. After all, research has suggested that "a single dinner at a professor's home, or a single focused conversation with a professor" can have an outsized impact on a student's success in college (Chambliss and Takacs 3). These interactions between students and faculty are already more likely to occur at SLACs than other institutions. But the professionalization and addition of student life offices should not discourage faculty from having multiple co-curricular interactions with their students. If anything, it should encourage faculty to collaborate more comprehensively with their colleagues in the student life office.

On the other hand, we find that the growth of administrative support services has also contributed to a consumerist culture that can make it more difficult for students to become forceful advocates for their own education. When students use administrative offices to avoid the challenges that come up as a matter of course in their classes, for example, their learning and agency are not advanced. Our learning spaces need to be ones in which students know they will be protected from discrimination or harassment, *and* where faculty know they will be given the room to explore the challenges that arise in those spaces without the fear that they will be hauled into a dean's office.

These challenges suggest the importance of creating multiple points of contact between critical student life offices and the faculty. As suggested above, faculty at SLACs need to take advantage of their schools' small size and invite student life professionals into conversations about curriculum, pedagogy, and student concerns, particularly those related to our attempts to create a culturally sustaining, inclusive, and equitable classroom.

Finally, SLACs must create a culture of collaborative autonomy that encourages responsibility and accountability on everyone's part, rather than adding to a disempowering, *in loco parentis* culture. Our goal is student empowerment, which can't be achieved by adding layers of rules and restrictions, or by substituting consumerism for responsibility.

Relations with Surrounding Communities

As proponents of an institutional culture that is collaborative, integrated, and fueled by a spirit of solidarity, we also see a strong need for campus-community interactions that are mutually respectful and beneficial. We are saddened that faculty and staff at our institutions have increasingly opted out of living and participating in our local communities, even if we understand why so many of them have made that decision. The residential element of our colleges pertains to all members of the campus community, and, while we certainly don't want to dictate how and where people should live, we believe that our newly envisioned hiring practices should intentionally address how potential faculty and administrators view their role as members of the local community.

In our view, a palpable element of the toxic culture we have been living in is the condescension or insensitivity that faculty and administrators sometimes show—wittingly or unwittingly—toward our local communities. For all of our talk of diversity and inclusion, we rarely acknowledge that "town-gown" tensions are exacerbated by an insensitivity to the economic realities of our community neighbors. We are excited about the potential of a truly reciprocal relationship between the college and its local community. Increasing the impact of community engagement should be a critical goal for SLACs, whether they do that through increased support given to community-based learning and research, efforts to increase dialogue and discussion between the town and the college, or the pursuit of projects that are mutually beneficial to both parties (for example, energy conservation projects, journalism students who can fill the gap in local news coverage as local papers disappear, support to K–12 education, or the shared use of athletic facilities).

Trustees

Ultimately, the changes we are proposing will only generate frustration and deadlock if an institution's trustees don't share the cultural and organizational approaches at the heart of this manifesto; we sincerely hope that we will be on the same page in most matters. Because most trustees are alumni, they provide the college with a valuable sense of institutional continuity, one that often stretches beyond the faculty's memory. They give generously of both their time and their resources to the colleges that, most will tell you, helped make them what they are today. But here's the rub: because they attribute their success to the colleges that they attended in years past, they can be wary of changing the institutions that, all said, worked exceptionally well for them. I (Steve) can't count the times that trustees shared with me their pleasurable remembrances of having been students in a history course of one of my now-departed colleagues, recounting how he—always a "he"—"lectured for fifty minutes nonstop and without a single note!" Full of praise for my colleague, I would try to gently glide the conversation into a discussion of research on the impact of active learning on student retention and engagement. The same reticence to change exists on a broader level. Trustees are often those most concerned with meritocratic rankings, especially how their college has fared in the latest *U.S. News* ranking, whether the SAT scores of incoming students are rising or falling, and if the college is getting the "best" students to apply. As representatives of the institution, trustees can be less than welcoming when students protest racist practices at their colleges, and they can be more attentive to the "snowflake" critique of today's students. Why can't they be like we were? is a frequent complaint.

The challenge faced by those of us concerned with changing the culture of our colleges is how to address the trustees' apprehensions in ways that they can hear, since their continued support is vital to our project. In the first place, we find it essential to establish open, two-way lines of communication between the trustees and other members of the college community. We would argue for increasing the opportunities faculty, staff, and students have to exchange ideas with trustees. And the more often these interactions can be conducted in small, facilitated sessions, rather than in large gatherings that frequently produce more heat than light, the better.

Secondly, we would suggest that it is highly useful to integrate trustees into the ongoing life of our colleges, and particularly into the teaching and learning activities that they relate to most strongly in their own experiences. If trustees retain the memory of the fifty-minute stand-up lecture as the embodiment of what teaching should be, the most powerful response would be to give them a seat in our classes today.

And not just in the occasional class session trustees can attend before their periodic on campus meetings, but as students, once again in our classes. If this was hardly possible in the past, since trustees tend to be spread across the country, our current digital reality has made this commonplace. I (Steve) actually did this a few years ago with alumni, adding ten graduates from the 1950s to the 2010s to an ongoing, in person, seminar. The alumni would join the class every week remotely, via conference presentation software, engaging in the discussions, and sharing their thoughts. The experience considerably changed, in a sharply positive fashion, how these alumni understood, and appreciated, the current generation of students.

Similarly, we would argue that trustees, and alumni in general, could be brought into the classroom in ways that vitalize the curriculum, as many work in cutting-edge fields. Years ago I (Beth) developed a course on non-profit management, sustainability, and social entrepreneurism that borrowed heavily from the course design of a business school model. Each meeting included a master class led by leading alumni and trustees in the field, with in-the-trenches expertise with the topic du jour. Students were never more engaged than they were in this class, hanging on every word of these former students who had applied the lessons they had learned in a liberal arts setting to all manner of industry. The key component, it seemed to me, was the willingness of the visiting trustees and alumni to truly "play" in the space alongside of the students—they were visibly committed to the students' success.

Finally, we recommend that one or more students be elected to serve as trustees, so as to insure that current student voices are represented in person to the board.

CLASSROOM CULTURE AND THE LEARNING ENVIRONMENT
Portraits of a Classroom (or, Why We Love Our Jobs)

Steve: *Long after other students had disappeared into their classes, mine stayed outside, clustered on the benches that lined the hallway. A passing faculty member eyed us curiously. Inside, a group of five students was rearranging the classroom as part of a midsemester project. In a course examining the rise and fall of dictatorships in the southern cone of South America in the 1960s and 1970s, we had turned to an exploration of why these regimes employed such brutal methods. Working in groups, students were allowed to use any modality to analyze how power works, and what, if any, were its limitations. This particular group, in an earlier discussion in my office, had suggested blindfolding their peers and leading them across campus to a semi-abandoned gym where their "captives" would be "interrogated." Power operates through fear, they explained, so a project that elicited fear would illuminate its meaning. In class, we had discussed extensively how traumatizing such experiences could be for those who studied them, let alone experienced them, and I raised these conversations again with the group. They took the matter to heart, reconsidered, and now we waited outside the classroom to see their reconceived project. When we finally entered, we saw that they had placed, on the floor and hanging from the ceiling, portraits of young people who had been "disappeared" in Argentina and Chile. The chalkboards were filled with quotes from the readings and details illustrating aspects of the lives of the young "disappeared" people. There was complete silence as we inched our way around, through, and under the images and stopped to read the commentary. And then a remarkable, chaotic conversation burst out as one student after another questioned the presenters about their choices, generating a discussion that left no one on the sidelines.*

Beth: *"An Existential Adventure."* That's the only thing the posters around campus and the advertisements in campus media outlets said. And yet, more than forty students came out to the oldest building on campus (legend says it's haunted) between 10:00 p.m. and midnight on a cold and dark December Tuesday to participate in a cryptic *"adventure,"* the culmination of our existential literature class. For seven weeks, the fifteen members of the class (with me only periodically guiding them) had been planning, taking on the challenge of creating an event that would bring a general audience into the conceptual space that we had been traveling through all semester. We started with several days of concept-mapping, a chance to synthesize the material—a whirlwind tour of the *"heavy hitters"* of existentialism—that we'd encountered during the first half of the semester. The second half of the semester was dedicated (in addition to the collaborative planning) to students expanding the conversation by bringing in new material that they found compelling and that was related in spirit to the questions we had been discussing. Each student led a session, challenging us to explore all manner of topics— from psychotropic drugs to climate change to xenophobia. Each conversation was more engaged and passionate than the next. That late Tuesday night—having landed on the idea that we wanted our general audience to come away with an experience that left people searching more deeply into themselves—the class members served as tour guides and performers. Our guests moved through (electric) candlelit hallways and a series of rooms. These included a *"waiting room,"* which forced people to contemplate what it means to *"wait"* for an undisclosed time and for an undisclosed outcome; a *"risk-taking"* room set up with a VR program that simulated walking a plank thirty stories high; and a *"gibberish room"* outfitted from floor to ceiling with all manner of random objects, white boards that posed existential questions that guests could answer, and class members in unsettling masks who silently interacted with guests in ways that broadcast how absurdity and *profundity coexist, and what it means to act when you don't know the code-breaking language. The rooms led through a maze to a drum circle, where our guests could experience bringing their individual voices into a collective conversation. In the hallways between stops, the tour guides led our guests in all manner of existential musings, asking them to weigh in on the relationship between personal autonomy and collective responsibility, to consider what freedom entails, and to think about what constitutes selfhood. For two hours on a dark and cold Tuesday night, they talked with one another about existentialism.*

We start with these two portraits because, for us, this is the heart of everything, why all of this is worth it. These experiences illustrate the sense of excitement and possibility, the charge that we've both experienced when a classroom comes to life in shared exploration, when a class of students collectively learns something they haven't known before. All classes, just as all faculty, are different, and they engage students in different ways. But we believe strongly in giving students the space they need to engage in creative and challenging conversations, and to discover who they are and who they can be. We would like to believe that most faculty members got into teaching in the first place because they know what these electric moments feel like when students take command of their own learning. What we're suggesting here are elements that can further this kind of classroom culture and learning environment that we have come to expect in the small liberal arts classroom, but that we don't always find.

The research is quite conclusive that pedagogies that encourage and promote students' active engagement in their own learning are more effective—in terms of retention, comprehension, and the ability to transfer what they learn from one domain to another—than a purely lecture-based model organized around the passive absorption of knowledge

(Barr and Tagg, Ambrose et al., Fink, Pascarella and Terenzini). Active learning, in this context, involves not only the acquisition of information, but metacognition, learning about one's own learning, as well. It also involves meaning-making and reflection in a systematic and disciplined way and in community with others. We find three broad concepts to be of particular importance when we think about creating a learning environment where this kind of experience can happen: 1) we have to create a culture of shared power and integrated learning; 2) we must establish culturally sustaining approaches that foreground lived experiences; and 3) we have to broaden our understanding of what constitutes expert knowledge.

1. Creating a Culture of Shared Power and Integrated Learning

A common characteristic in the two portraits above is that, in both cases, students directed the course of events within the context of the disciplinary or text-based frameworks we established and the learning goals we communicated. This is what we mean by "shared power"—everyone in the room has a hand in shaping the learning that happens, and the people in the room come to relate to each other as co-creators and partners in the production of new knowledge and their deeper understanding of existing knowledge. We recognize how ethereal that might sound, but we suggest that it is well-grounded in the world our students are entering. The days of the "sage on the stage" have come and gone. It never was a particularly robust learning model for many anyway, and now, as students face a knowledge economy where more of them will be engaged in entrepreneurial pursuits, this model is downright anachronistic. The truth—borne out well by the abrupt move to a virtual platform necessitated by the COVID-19 crisis and the challenges that many faculty faced during the transition—

is that most students have more technical and technological wherewithal than many faculty do to navigate this new economy. They also have grown up—for better or for worse—in a climate emphasizing career preparedness and an attendant set of expectations (i.e., internships, job shadowing) that have given them access to a sphere of experience that is wholly unfamiliar to many faculty members. Given the asymmetry of these assets, faculty are wasting an opportunity if they don't acknowledge the students' collective experience and then work to embed that experience into course design.

But it also requires creating a classroom culture that works to foster practices of democratic engagement: dialogue and deliberation based on informed reasoning, cultural inclusivity, engaged listening, and an awareness of the values that support learning communities. Now more than ever, these practices are a vital component of our classrooms that should be extended to the entire campus and the wider community. These practices complement the values of autonomy and integration that guide our recommendations for a revamped departmental structure and that mark the general culture of learning we envision. Everything we do in our classrooms should feed back into these values.

One of the more important developments in the process of making students equal partners in their learning is the model of student-faculty partnerships developed by Alison Cook-Sather at Bryn Mawr College. Partnerships, Cook-Sather and her coauthors argue, are "based on respect, reciprocity, and shared responsibility between students and faculty" (Cook-Sather et al. 1).

Student-faculty partnerships are now in place at many colleges both in the United States and abroad, including at Oberlin. Similar to practices at other colleges, students in Oberlin's program were paired with a faculty partner in a specific course in which they were not simultaneously enrolled. The students attended one class per week for the entire semester. They also met with their faculty partner at least once a week and with the program director and other students in the program on a regular basis. Students, who were paid for their time, provided faculty partners with feedback on an aspect of each class session that the faculty member was concerned about or that came to the attention of the student. Since the student partners were not enrolled in the classes they observed, they could become true collaborators, working with their faculty partners as they considered together how to deepen student learning. Students consistently derived new insights about the challenges of teaching. And faculty, for their part, were able to see their classes from a student's perspective, perhaps for the first time in their careers.

Many things make these partnerships work, but one important element is that student partners aren't enrolled in the course and therefore aren't being graded. Indeed, of the many factors that currently work against a learning culture characterized by responsibility, collaboration, and equity, the reliance on the common grading system that persists in most SLACs is close to the top, particularly as it plays out in faculty-student relations and the way it perpetuates a false meritocratic, assimilationist culture. It's a simple equation. In the context of a system where faculty power will always win, a culture of shared power will struggle to take root. And, as we've been arguing throughout, this is not a system that currently benefits anyone. Consider what the current grading system does to:

> **Students:** "Rather than motivating students to learn," Jeffrey Schinske and Kimberly Tanner conclude, "grading appears to, in many ways, have quite the opposite effect. Perhaps at best, grading motivates high-achieving students to

continue getting high grades—regardless of whether that goal also happens to overlap with learning. At worst, grading lowers interest in learning and enhances anxiety and extrinsic motivation, especially among those students who are struggling" (162). Think of the ways that current grading and assessment processes motivate counterproductive student behaviors like cheating (21 percent of Harvard seniors in 2016 self-reported as having cheated; and cheating scandals swept through the Air Force Academy in 2007, 2017, and 2019). Think of the students who will sacrifice creativity for the more assured higher grade.

Faculty: Think of those classes you've most dreaded going into, the ones where you suspect students are just there for the grade and could care less for the subject matter you're so passionate about. Think of the time you've spent deliberating between giving a paper an A- or a B+, or your decision to avoid collaborative assignments in order to prevent "free riders."

The Institution: An emphasis on grading, and the knowledge that a high GPA will help students enter the best graduate and professional schools, has produced a level of grade inflation that is, frankly, embarrassing (Rojstaczer). At Princeton, for example, a university that has actively tried to address the problem of grade inflation, the median grade during the 2018–2019 academic year was still an A-.

All of these examples describe a culture that is far more antagonistic than collaborative. Suspicions about a few students who might be gaming the system are squeezing out the potential for a far richer, more enjoyable experience for everyone.

A better approach would start from a growth-mindset ethos. It would encourage formative, rather than summative, assessment, and it would build student reflection into the assessment process. I (Beth) have developed a guided self-assessment method over the last eight years, for instance, that asks students to go through a rigorous reflective process for each element of the course. I provide each student with extensive qualitative feedback and a "suggested grade" for independent projects. Students then use those as a guide for determining their own grade. Students know from day one, via the learning contract on the syllabus and the assessment guidelines, what the assessment criteria will be and the role each criterion will play in the process. They know, too, that I "reserve the right to change the grade they've assigned to their performance, if my perception of their performance differs markedly from their own." This method has changed the entire experience of my classes, making them far more productive, energizing, and rigorous. There are a number of other approaches that can create a more authentic, meaningful, and student-directed experience than traditional grading, including peer assessment, contract grading (where students "contract" for particular grades, knowing the expectations of each), narrative or portfolio grading, and grading that rewards students for effort and participation (Swinton).

On a campus-wide level, colleges such as Hampshire and Bennington have moved away from standard letter grading altogether. At Bennington, for example, students receive detailed narrative evaluations for each course they take (they can receive an additional letter grade by request). This feedback helps a committee assess the student's proposed field of inquiry, and their progress in terms of specific areas: inquiry, research, creativity, engagement, and communication. The backbone of the process, however, is the student's self-assessment.

The fact that select campuses have adopted these methods suggests there is growing support for holistic practices that privilege student reflection and self-assessment. Changing the ways we grade student work also seems to make more sense for graduates who are going into the job market where, according to a *Forbes* survey, the top three most valued attributes of new hires are skills and culture fit, agility, and personality, not a high GPA. But even as research has shown that such approaches are associated with significant learning outcomes, they nevertheless are still widely viewed with suspicion. Even faculty who dislike current grading practices—are there any faculty members who *like* to grade?—argue that grading remains a necessity because without grades, students will be frozen out of the best professional schools and graduate programs.

Parents and students, if not those of us at SLACs ourselves, have to be appalled at the circular firing squad that's been created. Incessant testing and grades are needed in K–12 in order to determine who will get into a selective college, even though we know that these approaches are discriminatory and do not effectively measure or promote learning. Colleges then require yet more testing and grading so that their graduates will win a spot in a selective postgraduate program, even though we know grades detract from learning and add to everyone's anxiety. And graduate programs continue to turn out the next generation of faculty who say that we have always done it this way and can't change. But we can.

Similar to our suggestion that SLACs band together to reject *U.S. News*-type rankings, we believe that there has to be wholescale adoption of new assessment approaches that more authentically foster learning and encourage hard work.

2. Establishing Culturally Sustaining Approaches

Higher education has been a site for contesting racial inequality ever since the 1960s, when Black student activists rose up on campuses across the country as part of the broader civil rights movement. Since the murder of Trayvon Martin in 2012, antiracist protests have forced many colleges to consider their own relationship to a racist past and to examine current practices that sustain and propagate racism. There is a good reason for this. As Tressie McMillan Cottom argues, "It would be near impossible at almost any U.S. university to memorialize the institution's past without also memorializing the ideology of white nationhood and black subjugation" (Cottom 2015). Colleges and universities, including SLACs, began to address this some years ago by taking steps to increase the "compositional" diversity of their campus communities, admitting a more racially and ethnically diverse student body, and attempting to diversify the faculty and administrators. These steps have met with only limited success, however. They have been constrained by resentful white faculty exercising their privilege under an anti-affirmative action banner, and by admissions systems and hiring practices that, when run through the gears of meritocracy, continue to limit the pool of "qualified" candidates. One of the more unsettling products of this process has been the heated competition among elite schools for the disproportionately small number of students and faculty of color who have "succeeded" under the specific, limited terms recognized by the meritocratic system (Jack).

But as the current calls for dismantling racism and systems of oppression underscore, compositional diversity, in reality, is only the beginning of real systemic change. For students, faculty, or administrators of color, the more profound question is when they will be welcomed on their own culturally diverse terms and how institutions themselves will change. "Interactional" diversity speaks to issues of representation, accountability, and the value and significance of heritage practices, epistemologies, and community engagements, all elements that can provide (or refuse) access to opportunity and power (Brown McNair et al.).

The practices inherent in interactional diversity share broad affinities with the concept of culturally sustaining pedagogies (CSP) that educators have advanced in the context of K–12 schooling, although CSP is rooted in a more critical set of analytical approaches. (Not for the first time, K–12 educators, concerned as they must be with pedagogies, have opened the way for deeper thinking on the part of those of us in higher education.) Briefly, CSP sees multilingual and multicultural heritages and community practices as sources of strength; it demands explicitly pluralistic outcomes that move away from Eurocentric, monolingual/monocultural norms and notions of educational achievement; it works to raise students' abilities to critique dominant messages and regressive practices that privilege the status quo; and it requires teachers develop the capacity to apply these characteristics to their own practice. As the name implies, CSP maintains that it is not sufficient to teach a culturally relevant lesson or unit— to "just add women and stir," as feminist historians quipped when women's histories began to be added to textbooks in response to their critiques. Rather institutions must develop practices that *sustain* the valuation of a plurality of identities and cultures. Ultimately, Django Paris and H. Samy Alim write, CSP is about "a love that can help us see our young people as whole rather than broken . . . and a love that can work to keep them whole as they grow and expand who they are and can be through education" (14).

It is vital we extend CSP practices developed for K–12 students to our small liberal arts colleges. Until SLACs are able to critically examine and challenge the structures that sustain what W. E. B. DuBois conceptualized as the "double consciousness"—the sense of "always looking at one's self through the eyes of others, of measuring one's soul by the tape of a world that looks on in amused contempt and pity"—our colleges will never become welcoming places for all.

We cannot pretend that this is easy work; it is work that we ourselves have too long ignored and continually fall short of executing. But now, above all, is the "time for us to demonstrate how 'we learn with and from communities,'" as the dean of the University of Pittsburgh's School of Education, Valerie Kinloch, wrote to her campus in the wake of George Floyd's murder in May 2020. "Now is the time for our School community to wrestle with the history of Black pain and trauma, to determine how we have been complicit in that pain and trauma, and to learn with and from Black people as we seek to 'innovate and agitate.'" SLACs must take these challenges seriously, as we have argued, in terms of how they admit students, hire faculty, staff, and administrators, set goals, and evaluate their progress.

3. Broadening Our Understanding of What Constitutes Expert Knowledge

The persistent and relentless metrics-driven culture of assessment resembles a Möbius strip in terms of its insular focus on the task of "doing well" in school. The goal of faculty should instead be much more outward-focused; they should work with students to develop the skills and dispositions needed for broad-based success in life. The key principle we're advocating for is "high-road transfer," the application of knowledge or learning dispositions used in one domain to solve problems in different areas; skills that will allow them to be good in life, not just in school. In that sense, we want to move from a culture that too often seems to privilege knowledge for its own sake to a culture of embodied relevance (Milkova and Volk). For us, it's about fostering certain "habits of mind" (like collaboration, creative problem-solving, communication, critical thinking, dealing with ambiguity, and working across multiple disciplines and skill sets) that are useful both for being a member of the global workforce and for being a responsible and creative member of society. In the classroom, we think the development of these kinds of habits is driven by the premise that learning is an active, social process, one built on an understanding that living and learning must work in tandem, not in isolation.

In that spirit, we also believe that a central role of SLACs, and higher education in general, is to produce expert knowledge, and that each class should provide students with the opportunity for a dynamic push and pull between an engagement with existing artifacts of knowledge and the coproduction of new knowledge based on that engagement. But we worry that we are currently narrowing the sphere of possibility in our classrooms by too often privileging the academic path over all others, and too often marginalizing popular and alternative forms of scholarship based in orality, intergenerational knowledge, and social networking/social media (FitzPatrick Sifford and Cohen-Aponte). Faculty often remain tied to the narrow graduate programs that shaped so many of them. They tend to want to recreate students in their own image and to equate academic knowledge with rigor—but that happens to the great detriment of most students. Our new vision is informed instead by a basic principle of project-based learning, the idea that rigor and authenticity are enhanced when students are encouraged to work with and learn from practitioners of expert knowledge in multiple spheres. It's a model that acknowledges masters of their craft in all sectors, that motivates students to wrestle with course material in the service of becoming producers (rather than regurgitators) of knowledge, and that opens up new possibilities that students might not have previously considered.

Learning and Labor

To the extent that we are advocating for a learning culture that is experiential, collaborative, holistic, and authentic, we are intrigued by learning and labor models, and, particularly, by Berea College's "Labor Program." The program, one of Berea's "great commitments," is designed to "honor the dignity and utility of all work, mental and manual." Since 1906, every student at Berea must contribute at least seven hours per week (this was raised to ten hours in 1917) to the necessary work of the college. (Berea was modeled on Oberlin College which retains "Learning and Labor" as its official motto, although not its practice.) This "learning and labor" model captures for us, in many ways, the potential of a fully integrated residential approach, with its emphasis on "taking pride in work well done" as a concrete way to manifest the "productive restlessness" that will characterize this new culture. "Work," John Fee, Berea's founder, argued, "is the great equalizer," and this is particularly important in a context where there is a sharp divide in the student body between low-income students, who often have to work out of necessity, and higher-income students who don't. A requirement like this can help students reflect on their own privilege and consider the ways that intellectuals often dismiss those who engage in manual labor (Jack).

At the same time, we are cognizant of the fact that Berea's program is more than a century old and already firmly established as part of the school's mission. Instituting a similar program on other campuses today might also make many of the employment opportunities that are currently filled by residents from nearby communities redundant. In that sense, a move to replace local employees with student workers would undercut the broad-based community solidarity that is critical to this new model. Quite frankly, we don't know what the right answer is, but we raise the question in the hopes of stimulating a conversation with all stakeholders about how to implement a "mental and manual" work model in a way that does not take jobs away from others and that strengthens campus-community relations.

Finances: Making it Work

"The end is in the beginning and yet you go on," or so states Hamm in Samuel Beckett's absurdist one-act play, *Endgame*. It seems disturbingly appropriate for our current moment, set as it is in a post-apocalyptic future in which four characters attempt to make sense out of their lives while confined to a single room. After months of our own pandemic-imposed confinement, watching the death count rise and then reeling as cities and towns exploded after yet another police murder of yet another Black person, the apocalypse now feels closer than ever.

But Beckett's quote seems quite apposite in another way. We have put financial considerations at the end of our manifesto, not because they are unimportant, but because, as Rebecca Kolins Givan put it, "we should lead with our values, and our values should lead us." If all we stand for at the end of the day is maximizing revenue, what emerges from the pandemic's wreckage might not be worth saving. Too much of this kind of thinking is out and about these days, as analysts point to the ways colleges can cut costs without regard for their instructional programs or social missions. At the same time, we recognize that without a financial model, our proposals will be brushed away like so much lint on a jacket.

If it's not already apparent, we hasten to remind our readers that we are not economists. This particular gap in our resumes might become even more obvious as you read on. But after describing the value of the small liberal arts college and the power and potential it holds when it is reconceived through a radical imagination, we are compelled to offer some suggestions for both large and small steps that can get us closer to the goal of providing a quality liberal arts education for all who want it. To put it another way, these are steps that can help us approach a central goal: sustainable finances that can support need-blind admissions at all SLACs.

As complex as college finances are, some things about them are distressingly clear. A degree from a private liberal arts college is expensive. It is so expensive that relatively few families can swing it. This one truth, in turn, has driven three outcomes. In the first place, selective private colleges are drawing their students increasingly from the wealthiest tier of income earners, both from the United States and internationally. We can look at our own institutions, DePauw and Oberlin, for confirmation of this. As much as we love our schools, some of our numbers are concerning. The median family income of an Oberlin student is $178,000, and 70 percent of students come from the top 20 percent of income earners. The median family income of a DePauw student is $144,400, with 59 percent of students coming from the top 20 percent of income earners. And our two colleges are far from outliers in this regard (Economic Diversity).

The second outcome speaks to the economic benefits of a college degree. The opportunity costs of missing out on a college degree are significant. The average college graduate will earn about twice as much over her lifetime—an estimated $600,000 more—as the average high school graduate (Schanzenbach et al. 1). This is an economic advantage that multiplies dramatically as a student accumulates additional, particularly professional, degrees.

This substantial premium to the degree holder explains, in simple terms, the third outcome, the explosion of debt that families and students have taken on to pursue a college degree. Student loan debt, which stood at $772 billion in 2009, has doubled, soaring to $1.56 trillion in 2020, more than any other debt category in the United States except for mortgages.

The average student loan debt for students who graduated in 2018 may be north of $32,000, but lacking a degree will almost certainly guarantee a low-income future. So the debts continue to accumulate.

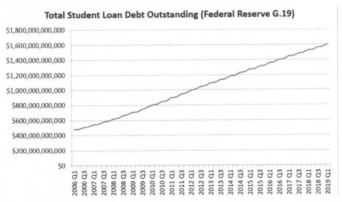

Source: Federal Reserve Board

We have no quarrel with those who point out that this path is unsustainable. Continue along it and SLACs will become even more privileged clubs than they are already, and fewer of them will survive. We have suggested a number of practices and assumptions that have brought us to this point. But, it is also important to be clear about the financial realities of higher education, particularly at small liberal arts colleges, that have pushed SLACs out of reach for most low-income families, as those realities are not always well-known.

To begin, we need to talk about price and cost before suggesting some ways out of this thicket. Let's start with price and the difference between "sticker" and "discount" pricing. For the 2016–17 academic year, tuition, fees, room, and board at four-year, private, nonprofit institutions averaged around $45,000. That's the "sticker price." It's what you see when you visit a college's website, and it's what pundits cite when they rail about the high price of college. But that price is not what everyone pays. In reality, the average family actually paid about $26,000 for the 2016–17 academic year. That's still expensive (nearly half of the income of a median family), but not *as* expensive. It's more in the range of a Buick than an Audi Q5.

The difference between the two figures is the "discount rate," a percentage which takes into account all forms of financial aid. In 2018, the discount rate at 405 private, nonprofit colleges and universities was more than 52 percent. This means that, on average, the price of a private college education was less than half of what was advertised (Valbrun). At Oberlin, for example, the total sticker price for tuition, room, board, and fees for 2017–18 was just under $75,000, but the average net price was under $40,000. Grants averaged about $28,000, and about 83 percent of the students received some financial support. Again, that price is still out of the range of most people, but not as heart-stoppingly expensive as it is at first glance. And we can put these figures into further perspective by reminding that SLACs are characterized by their small class size and the personalized attention they offer from faculty at the top of their fields. At UCLA, where out-of-state tuition in 2020-21 was $42,994, about half of their classes have 20 students or fewer. At nearby Pomona ($54,380), more than 70 percent of the classes have 20 students or fewer.

So, why don't colleges just advertise their "real" (discount or net) price and charge the same for everyone? As elite as many colleges have become, they still remain one of the few Robin Hood institutions in the United States. Income from the wealthy is redistributed in the form of financial aid down the income chain. If Oberlin charges everyone $40,000, they have just lost $35,000 from families who can afford it to help support those who can't (Koch). Of course, not every institution uses the difference between the full and the discount price to support financial aid, and there are also a variety of mechanisms, primarily merit aid—a grotesque by-product of meritocratic competition—that wealthier families can take advantage of to avoid this "wealth tax." In order to boost their rankings in the *U.S. News* sweepstakes, colleges offer generous aid packages to attract students who will bring their accomplishments with them: SAT scores, high GPAs, high school science competition wins, and coveted spots as first chair in the state's youth orchestra. Students who do well in high school will be offered merit scholarships whether or not they demonstrate financial need.

Finally, there is one other aspect of a college's high sticker price that is targeted to those enfolded in the prestige economy: down-market doesn't sell. If it doesn't cost a lot, the thinking goes, it's probably not worth a lot. A pour-over coffee at $7.50, which takes twenty minutes to prepare, speaks to the consumer's taste, discernment, and expertise, even if that same customer could get a good brew for $1.25 at the local bodega. It's exactly the same with college diplomas.

But price isn't cost. Why does college *cost* so much? And why has tuition increased faster than the cost of other goods? In the public sphere, where tuition is rising at a faster rate than at private colleges, the answer is fairly clear. Tuition has risen to compensate for the withdrawal of state aid. But what about costs at private colleges? To answer that question adequately would require more expertise than we have and more pages than we are allotted here. But here are a few simple, but illustrative, answers. In the first place, while salaries and benefits at private liberal arts colleges have increased over the past four decades, the increase has not been excessive. It certainly is nothing like the surge in salaries for other professionals (doctors, lawyers, engineers, Division I football coaches), or in the corporate sector in general. And whatever salary hikes the faculty have enjoyed since the 1970s stopped with the Great Recession. Between

2008 and 2020, average real salaries of full-time faculty at all ranks at baccalaureate colleges were flat (AAUP-2020, 5). Additions to the administrative ranks were far more significant in terms of a college's overall expenses. Academic support (administrative costs) jumped tenfold between 1980 and 2015, climbing from $13 billion to $122.3 billion as colleges took on more tasks (Simon). Technology costs have also greatly increased over the last few decades; they now consume nearly 5 percent of undergraduate budgets. That probably will only increase in our likely online future. Finally, universities, even at the undergraduate level, have seen increasing costs for library materials and database access, the cost of scientific equipment, and the price of labs. Start-up labs, a typical part of a salary offer in the sciences, for example, can cost as much as $1.5 million. Before you know it, we're talking about real money, as they say.

So one reason behind higher education's swelling price tag is that it actually costs a lot to mount a robust educational program. So perhaps a better question to ask is whether the tuition and fees that students pay actually go to support their education (i.e., instruction), or whether those dollars are consumed by lazy rivers, football scoreboards, or Starbucks franchises. We can start again by examining the two institutions where we teach. In 2016–17, DePauw took in $41 million from tuition and fees and spent $49.5 million on instruction; Oberlin brought in $90.2 million in tuition and fees while spending $89.2 on instruction. Williams, one of the wealthiest SLACs, received $68.4 million in tuition and fees and expended over $100.5 million for instructional purposes (Colleges That Spend). In other words, as high as tuition and fees at SLACs are, they only account for a portion of what an *education* actually costs. The rest is made up largely by endowment-generated funds, grants, and fundraising.

Other institutions spend far less of their tuition income on instruction. Liberty University in Virginia, for example, generated almost $700 million from tuition and fees in 2016–17 while spending only $174.4 million on instruction. Southern New Hampshire University vacuumed up $598.4 million from students while spending $111.4 million on instruction. As we argued above, if our goal was simply to find a financing model that would keep SLACs solvent, such models are available, and they are usually based on driving up class size and driving down faculty compensation. But if we are looking to sustain an institution that can provide a meaningful education and that can prepare students for a complex future, we need to look beyond solvency. To be sure, there are costs that need to be controlled and expenditures that should be stopped. But ultimately, we need to build a financial model that supports the kind of education our students—all students—deserve.

So, how can this work in a way that makes small liberal arts colleges *available* to everyone who wants this kind of education? How can we make all SLACs, not just those with the largest endowments, *need-blind?* We must take some steps at our own institutions. But to be honest, there are also some actions that have to occur in the public sphere, where the political and economic structures that have defunded education for over four decades must be upended. The power to rewrite those rules is there if we take it.

There are three ways to think about what can be done: 1) we can extend existing models and introduce new ones; 2) we can decrease costs, guided by the principle of community solidarity and a refusal to view the immiseration of faculty or staff as a "solution" to financial problems; and 3) we can change public policy regarding higher education.

1. Extending Current Funding Models; Introducing New Models

Alumni Giving

One of the unique features of higher education in the United States is the degree to which college graduates identify with their undergraduate institutions and will support them financially. Generational loyalties in Europe are often fiercely linked to a particular football club; in the United States, those loyalties tend to belong to a university. And at private colleges and universities, more so than at public ones, alumni support has long been a major tool in narrowing the gap between price and cost. In that regard, it is the small liberal arts colleges, not the Division I athletic powerhouses, that generate the most consistent alumni devotion. In 2018, out of the top fifty higher educational institutions in terms of the percentage of alumni giving, thirty-two were SLACs (including eight of the top ten) (Hansen). It's not the football team at Claremont-McKenna (which was ranked sixth on the alumni-giving list) or the basketball squad at Wellesley (ranked eighth) that has engendered such fierce loyalty. Above all else, it is the entire college experience and the alumni's close connections to the faculty.

Still, there is not one school on the list of 200 colleges and institutions where the rate of alumni giving surpasses 50 percent. The average among the top ten schools is only 41 percent. The financing model that we are envisioning is one that draws on a deeper commitment from alumni who embrace the new mission of the radically reimagined institution. It is our hope that liberal arts institutions—those that are bold enough to take risks and build into every structure and practice the values that the college has long maintained but all too often sacrificed to the ranking-system gods or expediency—will generate greater support from current and future alumni. This change will not come automatically. Instead, it will require SLACs to engage in extended, transparent conversations about the ways they can establish themselves as exemplary models of inclusion and equity and best position themselves in the higher education universe.

Pay-It-Backward and Income-Sharing Models

Income Sharing Agreements (ISA), also known as "pay-it-backward" or deferred payment models, are beginning to influence how families plan for the cost of a college degree. In a standard ISA, such as Purdue's "Back a Boiler" plan, students defer tuition payments until after they graduate, at a rate based on a percentage of their presumed income for a set period of time. Typically, this rate is in line with a private student loan, but it is interest free. Because the payment is linked to a future salary, it deliberately aligns the cost and value of the student's education. When the prescribed term of the agreement is completed, the loan is terminated, whether or not the recipient paid less (or more) than the amount of support they received.

In the post-pandemic SLAC, we envision an even more comprehensive approach to the deferred payment plan, basing it on a graduate's actual (rather than projected) salary. Payments would also stop when the original amount has been repaid or the terms of the contract have been satisfied. We also recommend that ISA-style deferred payments be forgiven if the graduate completes a specific number of years in the employment of public service or nonprofit work, much like the federal loan-forgiveness policy we suggest below.

While it is too soon to know whether ISAs are succeeding in reducing costs and increasing access to higher education, they have raised concerns in some sectors regarding students who defer payment but never graduate. Given the higher four- and six-year graduation rates at small liberal arts colleges, this is one reason why ISAs might be a useful financial tool for parents and students, particularly if they are employed to "close the gap" that other grants might not cover. With their emphasis on having graduates—now viable members of the workforce who can appreciate the concrete value of their education—contribute to their own education, ISAs could generate increased enthusiasm, and a higher giving rate, from alumni, and donations could be aimed specifically at funding the program until it is self-sustaining.

Endowment-Based Tuition Reduction Models

The vast majority of SLACs regularly draw income from their endowments to help narrow the gap between price and cost. On average, 22 percent of private colleges' budgets comes from endowment income. As of 2018, twelve colleges had endowments that surpassed $1 billion; another ten had endowments in the $900 million range (Which Colleges). Among those toward the top stands Berea, which has a $1.2 billion endowment. Berea is notable in many ways, including its commitment to learning and labor, which we have already referenced (Harris 2018a). But it is also exceptional among SLACs in that 85 to 90 percent of its students are eligible for federal Pell Grants, which are awarded solely based on a student's financial need. But most conspicuous is the fact that Berea has been tuition-free since 1892. That doesn't mean that it doesn't *cost* anything to attend, just that students don't pay tuition. Berea actually costs $54,866 a year in tuition, but all students receive a $35,100 tuition grant and are paid $9,000 as a "labor grant," which leaves a bill of $10,766 for room and board and other fees and expenses. The college, therefore, pays out yearly from its endowment and other funds to absorb the tuition of its 1,670 students. And Berea isn't the only tuition-free college in the country. Cooper Union (which has an endowment of $826 million) had been tuition-free from its founding in 1902 until 2014, and it recently announced its decision to gradually return to a no-tuition stance by 2029; it already discounts its sticker price by some 76 percent.

So why shouldn't we argue for a tuition-free model at all SLACs, a model many people are proposing for public institutions of higher education? As we have said, the simplest answer is that only a few colleges have a large enough endowment to support that type of program. It's simply not an option available to the Utica Colleges of the country, those with endowments below $25 million, for example. There are other reasons why a tuition-free model is not as appealing as it sounds. As we have already suggested, colleges generate financial aid dollars through students who pay full price. Given Berea's larger endowment, the no-tuition model makes financial sense. But it also makes moral sense, given the school's decision many years ago to admit students almost exclusively from low-income, Appalachian families. But that model won't work for all schools. And since there really is no scenario in which a tuition-free model would be realistic at all SLACs, what we are pursuing instead is a financial model that can support *need-blind admission* at all SLACs. So how can we get there?

The median endowment for schools ranked by *U.S. News* is $65.1 million. But there are a number of colleges with endowments over $500 million, and the first question we raise is whether those institutions could be using their endowments to increase accessibility for low-income families. A 2016 report by The Education Trust—pre-COVID-19, to be sure—argued that they could (Nichols and Santos).

Few investment managers will advise colleges to draw more than 5 percent from their endowment funds in order to pay for current expenses; most of them are even more conservative.

The Education Trust examined whether those colleges in the $500 million endowment club who were drawing less than 5 percent a year from their endowments could enroll more low-income students if they merely raised their draw to that still-conservative level. Of the thirty-five institutions in this group, thirteen are SLACs. If these institutions raised their endowment draw to 5 percent, they could each pay for, on average, thirty-eight additional low-income students per year. If they raised their endowment draw to 5.5 percent, with the explicit purpose of funding need-blind admissions, the numbers would rise accordingly. The COVID-19 shutdown is prompting many colleges to increase their payout rates and use extraordinary withdrawals to get through the next few years. But when finances return to more normal levels, as we expect they will at some point, the proposal to increase endowment payouts for the explicit purpose of moving toward need-blind admissions should be seriously considered.

2. Decreasing Costs

By moving away from a competitive model based on chasing after meritocratic gold rings, SLACs can devote more funds toward need-based aid. Other discussions of cost-saving measures, based on community input from all sectors, including students, can identify areas where savings can be generated. But as a start, we can outline three recommendations for small liberal arts colleges that will allow them to prioritize the use of resources for need-based aid.

End Merit (Non-Need) Scholarships
One study found that between 2001 and 2017, public four-year universities spent nearly $32 billion of their own

financial aid dollars, about $2 out of every $5, on students whom the federal government deemed were able to afford college without financial aid (Burd 5). The purpose behind merit aid is crystal clear: "For schools like the University of Alabama, Miami University of Ohio, and Temple University," according to the College Board, "there has been no more important goal than rising up the *U.S. News & World Report* national university rankings." And one way to do that is to entice "attractive" students with merit scholarships. At private universities, students from families with annual earnings higher than $155,000 receive, on average, $5,800 more per year in financial support than a federal formula says they need. We do not have comparable figures for all small liberal arts colleges, but some evidence suggests that these amounts can add up quickly. The value of merit scholarships at Guilford College ranges from $20,000 to $80,000 over four years. Kenyon College offers $15,000 renewable scholarships to "outstanding students whose academic achievement, leadership potential, and accomplishments in activities place them in the top 10 to 15 percent of admitted students." DePauw offers merit scholarships based on the quality of high school courses taken, "with specific attention paid to honors, AP and IB courses completed," GPA, class rank, and SAT/ACT scores. Occidental College offers merit scholarships to "a limited number of incoming students who have demonstrated the highest level of academic achievement and will continue this success at Oxy." The list goes on. That these awards are driven by a desire to move up in the national rankings is at least indicated, if not confirmed, by the fact that colleges at the top of the charts, and those with the largest endowments, offer few or no merit scholarships.

Amenities

By and large, SLACs do not build lazy rivers or expend millions of dollars on electronic scoreboards, although they often do invest in other costly capital projects. And they compete with each other for students on the basis of student amenities, including housing, higher quality dining hall food, swank student unions and, on occasion, Starbucks outlets. A sample of 1,300 four-year public and private nonprofit higher education institutions found that they spent an average of $0.51 on consumption amenities for every dollar spent on academics, with wealthier students being more willing to pay for the "good things in life" (Jacob et al.). A much-referenced podcast by Malcolm Gladwell compared Vassar's lower spending on housing and food to that of Bowdoin, arguing that, because of its decision to cut back on the "luxuries," Vassar could admit more Pell-eligible students than Bowdoin, with its down-east lobster bakes. Gladwell's story has been heavily criticized; the differences in expenditures between the two schools are actually minimal, and Vassar can hardly afford to let its facilities deteriorate to such a degree that it can no longer compete for high-income students. Still, as Vassar's former president observed, "When we compete with each other, it pushes up costs. We do cool things, but it costs more money" (Blumenstyk). If Bowdoin spent $1,000 less per student on food, according to Robert Kelchen, a professor who studies college costs, they could admit "11 or so new low-income students." That's not a large number ... unless you are one of those eleven students. But more to the point, SLACs should be competing on the basis of their mission and their academic program, not on housing, food, or proverbial climbing walls.

Athletics

As part of the NCAA's Division III, SLACs spend considerably less on varsity sports than Division I schools. The median expenses of a Division III school with a football team were $4.1 million in 2019-20. By way of comparison, Ohio State spent a little more than $210 million (and Dabo Swinney, Clemson's head football coach, walked away with a tidy $9.3 million). Division III schools do not offer athletics scholarships, although nearly three-quarters of Division III student-athletes receive some form of merit- or need-based financial aid. Still, it would be easy to argue that SLACs can save money by cutting, or limiting, their varsity sports and focusing instead on club or intramural sports. And such a step should be considered for those sports that consistently fail to generate local enthusiasm or attract student-athletes. And it should most definitely be considered for football, not (necessarily) because the programs are more expensive than other sports, but in response to the well-documented studies of traumatic brain injuries that are an integral part of tackle football (Bachynski). We have seen our share of student-athletes hobble into class on crutches or with their arms in a sling, but sports that have been shown to cause permanent damage to some players should not have a place on SLAC campuses.

But athletics at all levels, particularly when seen through a health and wellness framework, are an important component in our holistic vision of the student. For many students who have no desire to become professional athletes, the opportunity to play on a varsity team is precisely why they decide to attend a small liberal arts college. And there is an abundance of research to suggest that this is a good choice for the student and the college alike. Student-athletes have a higher graduation rate than non-athletes and self-report as being more involved in campus activities and off-campus volunteering than non-athletes. Not surprisingly, given the amount of time that they need to devote to their sport, studies indicate that they are better than their peers at time management. If anything, and as suggested above, we would argue for a closer integration between academics and athletics at the level of student learning. What students are learning via physical activity, team sports, or individual competition not only impacts their learning in other domains. The dispositions they can develop via athletics—resilience, self-awareness, communication, collaboration, empathy, discipline, self-control—will likely increase their chances for success when they graduate (Bowen and Levin).

3. Public Policy and Private Colleges

The remarkable growth of the United States in the twentieth century was underwritten, in many respects, by a higher education system that most people could afford. Tuition remained quite low at land grant universities until the 1970s. Governor Ronald Reagan began to defund the University of California system in the mid-1970s, arguing that taxpayers should not "subsidize intellectual curiosity." The City University of New York system was free until 1976. As state legislatures began to defund higher education, the burden fell on the backs of families who have increasingly been unable to bear the burden, particularly as the minimum wage has remained fixed at a punishingly low level since 1968. A disregard for higher education at any time is shortsighted. But at a time when our very lives depend on the knowledge produced in these institutions—consider not just the current COVID-19 pandemic, but the climate crisis already upon us—such negligence must be recognized as nothing less than suicidal.

Change Fiscal Policy to Support Higher Education

Higher education is an essential public good, one that is provided by both public and private colleges and universities. Together, they compose the educational infrastructure which, quite literally, will determine the country's future. The value that is returned to the local, state, and national community by the skills and knowledge individuals gain in higher education does not discriminate by whether it was fostered in a public or a private institution of higher learning. When your child is vaccinated for measles, the pediatrician doesn't say, "This vaccine was created by scientists at Berkeley/Yale." They just give your kid the shot.

A new willingness to tax high-income earners at the state level will restore desperately needed funds to public higher education, allowing for free public education at community colleges and free or low-cost education at state schools. But changes in fiscal policy at the federal level can support private higher education as well. To the extent that private colleges, including SLACs, provide for the public good, we advocate for a funding model where the cost of attending a private college would be discounted by the cost of a public education and provided to students on a sliding-scale basis where higher-income families pay more.

Expand and Extend Pell Grants

In 1980, a Pell Grant on average covered approximately 80 percent of college costs (tuition, fees, and room and board). Now it only covers 29 percent. The Obama administration expanded these grants in 2009; they need to be expanded further as an important means of reversing the rise in income inequality in the country. Congress should double the size of a Pell Grant (it is currently set at a $6,345 maximum) and extend the income qualification in order to reach more middle-income families who currently can't access federal support but who also can't afford to pay for college. The government currently spends $28 billion on Pell Grants, which went to nearly 8 million undergraduates in 2017. By way of comparison, the government spends about $80 billion a year to keep 2.3 million people in federal prisons. *One* Gerald R. Ford-class aircraft carrier costs $13 billion. It's a classic choice between guns and butter. An aircraft carrier will not save us from a pandemic or help reverse climate change. Education could.

Tax Endowments to Encourage Low-Income Admissions

As private institutions, SLACs are public charities, and therefore they are not taxed. Yet they are part of broader fiscal planning measures that are (or should be) intended to serve the public good. One can be forgiven for thinking that Congress began to address this inequity in the 2017 tax bill by slapping a tax on endowments above a certain ceiling, but the provision was more likely a populist swipe at so-called liberal universities. Be that as it may, in 2019, Stanford faced a $42 million tax bill on its $27.7 billion endowment. But Congress *can* write tax policies that serve a public purpose with regard to private colleges and universities.

As it did in the 2017 act, Congress should tax colleges or universities with endowments over a stipulated amount (say, $500 million). These wealthy institutions, which have increasingly become private clubs for high-income families, have benefited from tax policies that low- and middle-income families have paid for. But institutions that enroll a significant percentage of Pell-eligible students should be exempt from this tax. Admitting more low-income students, particularly if the size of Pell Grants was increased as recommended above, would serve the public good and encourage those small liberal arts colleges with large endowments to increase the number of low-income students they enroll.

National Service Bill

We urge legislation that authorizes a newly conceived "National Service Bill" for higher education that is more in tune with our current reality. The legislation would be based on the post-9/11 GI Bill, which pays up to $25,162.14 per academic year at private colleges. Colleges that participate in the add-on "Yellow Ribbon" program enter into a voluntary agreement with the Department of Veterans Affairs to waive a portion of, or all, the tuition costs that exceed the national maximum; the agency then matches the amount of the waiver. As opposed to the two previous GI Bills, a reconceived bill would also be available to people who are employed in a variety of occupations considered to be of national service and in the public interest, including teaching, public health, community organizing, and caregiving for both the young and the elderly. A National Service Bill would not only aid SLACs financially, but it would also encourage a wider diversity of students to apply for admission. This new model would give attention to race and ethnicity (particularly important as the original GI Bill discriminated against Black servicemen), but also to considerations of class and, importantly, life experience.

Education Enhancement Tax

In addition, we would recommend that Congress pass an "education tax" on all corporations with sales above a certain threshold. The funds generated would be passed on to students enrolled in any accredited college or university. Higher education has been increasingly directed toward workforce development and serving the "needs of the market." These pressures are even felt at small liberal arts colleges where, we are told, we must align more consciously with corporate needs. But of course, when students take out loans to finance their education to get a job dictated by market needs, it is they, not their potential employers, who are left holding the debt if the job they are training for vanishes. This new "education enhancement tax" would be modeled along the lines of the UK's apprenticeship levy, which requires all employers with an annual payroll of more than £3 million ($3.71 million) to pay a tax of 0.5 percent of their payroll on apprenticeships, with the government kicking in an extra 10 percent "top-up" to those apprenticeship funds. This type of "education enhancement tax," available to all students, would recognize that if the corporate world in general is to benefit from the workforce development higher education provides, it should also absorb some of the risks and costs.

Increase the Minimum Wage
Finally, we come full circle. We have argued that a family's need to resort to debt in order to finance a college education has been driven by three factors: rising costs, regressive fiscal policies, and the stagnation of wages. Above, we have addressed some of the ways to control costs, as well as the larger need for a radical approach to fiscal policy that addresses the importance of higher education for the country's future. But we also must address a third factor. Income inequality is the hallmark of the neoliberal economy, and it has been driven by an insistence that the US economy cannot compete internationally unless it drives down wages at home. Forty years later, the argument has to be restated for what it really has meant. The rich cannot get even richer unless the poor get even poorer. Simply put, no democracy can survive for long under those terms. The financial crisis of higher education will not be solved until workers are treated with dignity and compensated fairly.

"America," Marilynne Robinson writes, "is the most powerful economy in history and at the same time so threatened by global competition that it must dismantle its own institutions, [including] the educational system. . . . This richest country has been overtaken with a deep and general conviction of scarcity, a conviction that has become an expectation, then a kind of discipline, even an ethic" (2020). Ever since the 1970s, and with very little pushback, higher education has been starved of needed support under the "conviction of scarcity." State and local politicians, almost *every one* of them a college graduate, warn of the dangers that will befall us should we consider even slowing down the rate of *increase* of funding to the military, police, or carceral system. Yet they have not blinked while cutting the legs out from under our (and presumably, their) children's education. These policies have been harmful for both public and private higher education. Regressive federal tax and wage policies have benefited the rich, squeezed the middle class, and crushed the poor. And they have pushed SLACs onto an unsustainable path of relying on an ever-smaller number of wealthy families.

Can we change? "Historically," as Arundhati Roy wrote, "pandemics have forced humans to break with the past and imagine their world anew." And this crisis is no different. The crisis moment has already brought about radical changes that none thought were possible even weeks before. Require all educational institutions to shift to online instruction, and do it in two weeks? Make the SAT/ACT optional for college admission? Remove the Confederate battle standard from the Mississippi state flag? Rename the Woodrow Wilson School of Public and International Affairs at Princeton? All done. Bettina Love, a professor of educational theory and practice at the University of Georgia, marveled at how changes that K–12 educators have demanded for decades suddenly materialized in the midst of the pandemic. Schools shut down, and as she notes, "in a matter of a month, we're done with standardized testing." Educators, belittled for years by state legislators, were suddenly being recognized for the important work they do every day. "Teacher, we need you. We're going to rely on your pedagogy and your ingenuity, and your creativity during this time." School superintendents started to argue for "compassion over compliance." Love's main point is this: now that we know what is possible, we're not going back (Abolitionist Teaching 57:55).

But will we change? As the summer of 2020 heats up and the country navigates its way through an unrelenting pandemic and the much older burden of anti-Black racism, colleges are attempting to prepare for a fall semester without knowing who will come or how they will be taught, fed, or housed. But one thing is clear: we can't stay where we are. This is the moment for radical change, the moment to accept the challenge to become the institutions that we should be, the moment to "disorder the disorder." It is our firm belief and ardent hope that we will *learn* ourselves out of these crises and that small liberal arts colleges, as they have before, will play a critical part in this. Now is the time to seize back the power we have given away. That goes for those of us who work at small liberal arts colleges who have let *U.S. News* and the prestige economy make our decisions for us; for those of us in higher education who have allowed the corporate demand to be competitive in the global economy determine our purpose; and for those of us who have accepted the defunding of education in return for accumulating an ever-higher mountain of personal debt. All of us, together, are in the crisis of our lifetimes. Let's not let it go to waste.

References

AAUP. https://www.aaup.org/sites/default/files/2019-20_survey_tables_2.pdf.

AAUP-2020. "The Annual Report on the Economic Status of the Profession, 2019–20." May 2020, https://www.aaup.org/sites/default/files/2019-20_ARES.pdf.

"Abolitionist Teaching and the Future of Our Schools," https://www.youtube.com/watch?v=uJZ3RPJ2rNc&feature=share&fbclid=IwAR28fz7R-Yd6UZpQLp98wV39xbseeVdRMuk9Oh1fTe6Z11Lsw3vA6PRalMU.

Algar, Selim. "Poverty rate soars among NYC schoolkids." *New York Post*, October 29, 2018, https://nypost.com/2018/10/29/poverty-rate-soars-among-nyc-schoolkids/.

Als, Hilton. "My Mother's Dreams for Her Son, and All Black Children." *New Yorker*, June 21, 2020, pp. 18-23.

Ambrose, Susan A. et al. *How Learning Works*. Jossey-Bass, 2010.

Arum, Richard, and Josipa Roksa. *Academically Adrift: Limited Learning on College Campuses*. Chicago, 2011.

Association of American Universities. "AAU Releases 2019 Survey on Sexual Assault and Misconduct," October 15, 2019, https://www.aau.edu/newsroom/press-releases/aau-releases-2019-survey-sexual-assault-and-misconduct.

Bachynski, Kathleen. *No Game for Boys to Play: The History of Youth Football and the Origins of a Public Health Crisis*. University of North Carolina Press, 2019.

Barr, Robert B., and John Tagg. "From Teaching to Learning. A New Paradigm for Undergraduate Education." *Change*, vol. 27, no. 6, November/December 1995, pp. 12-23.

Barrett-Fox, Rebecca. March 12, 2020, https://anygoodthing.com/2020/03/12/please-do-a-bad-job-of-putting-your-courses-online/.

Blumenstyk, Goldie. "Will Higher Ed's 'Culture' Help Colleges Navigate Their Future? Or Make It Tougher?" *Chronicle of Higher Education*, May 27, 2020, https://www.chronicle.com/article/Will-Higher-Ed-s/248853?cid=wcontentlist_hp_latest.

Bowen, William G., and Sarah A. Levin. *Reclaiming the Game: College Sports and Educational Values*. Princeton University Press, 2005.

Bowman, Nicholas A., and Michael N. Bastedo. "Getting on the Front Page: Organizational Reputation, Status Signals, and the Impact of *U.S. News and World Report* Rankings on Student Decisions." *Research in Higher Education*, vol. 50, no. 5, 2009, pp. 415–436.

Bradley, Stefan M. "No One Escapes Without Scars." *Chronicle of Higher Education Review*, April 18, 2019, https://www.chronicle.com/interactives/20190418-black-academic?utm_source=at&utm_medium=en&utm_source=Iterable&utm_medium=email&utm_campaign=campaign_1310349&cid=at&source=ams&sourceId=30292.

Brown, Joshua, et al. "The Hidden Structure: The Influence of Residence Hall Design on Academic Outcomes." *Journal of Student Affairs Research and Practice*, vol. 56, no. 3, 2019, pp. 267-283.

Brown McNair, Tia, et al. *Becoming a Student-Ready College: A New Culture of Leadership for Student Success*. Jossey-Bass, 2016.

Burd, Stephen. "Crisis Point: How Enrollment Management and the Merit-Aid Arms Race Are Derailing Public Higher Education." *New America*, February 2020, https://d1y8sb8igg2f8e.cloudfront.net/documents/Crisis_Point_2020-02-10_FINAL.pdf.

Calderon, Valerie J., et al. "Confidence in U.S. Public Schools Rallies." *Gallup News*, September 14, 2017, https://news.gallup.com/poll/219143/confidence-public-schools-rallies.aspx.

Carnegie Classification of Institutions of Higher Education. "2018 Update: Facts & Figures," 2019, https://carnegieclassifications.iu.edu/downloads/CCIHE2018-FactsFigures.pdf.

Catolico, Eleanore. "In a city with high poverty rates, the Detroit district will hand out meals during the school closure." *Chalkbeat Detroit*, March 13, 2020, https://detroit.chalkbeat.org/2020/3/13/21195978/in-a-city-with-high-poverty-rates-the-detroit-district-will-hand-out-meals-during-the-school-closure.

Chambliss, Daniel F., and Christopher G. Takacs. *How College Works*. Harvard, 2014.

Chick, Nancy, et al. "Distinctive Learning Experiences: Can we identify the signature pedagogies of residential liberal arts institutions?" May 12, 2020, http://blogs.rollins.edu/endeavor/2020/05/12/distinctive-learning-experiences-can-we-identify-the-signature-pedagogies-of-residential-liberal-arts-institutions/.

Chronicle Data. Https://data.chronicle.com/category/ccbasic/21/staff-salaries/.

Chronicle of Higher Education. *Almanac 2019-20*, vol. LXV, 2020.

Clauset, Aaron, et al. "Systematic inequality and hierarchy in faculty hiring networks." *Sciences Advances*. February 12, 2015, https://advances.sciencemag.org/content/1/1/e1400005.

College Board. "Trends in Student Aid Highlights – 2019," https://research.collegeboard.org/trends/student-aid/highlights.

"Colleges That Spent Far Less or More on Instruction Than They Brought In in Tuition and Fees, 2016-17." *The Chronicle of Higher Education*, July 14, 2019, https://www.chronicle.com/article/Colleges-That-Spent-Far-Less/246669.

Collins, Chuck, et al. "Billionaire Bonanza 2020: Wealth Windfalls, Tumbling Taxes, and Pandemic Profiteers." *Inequality*, April 23, 2020, https://inequality.org/great-divide/billionaire-bonanza-2020/.

Cook-Sather, Alison, et al. *Engaging Students as Partners in Learning and Teaching*. Jossey-Bass, 2014.

Cottom, Tressie McMillan. "Injustice at Universities Runs Deeper Than Names." *The Atlantic*, October 26, 2015, https://www.theatlantic.com/politics/archive/2015/10/injustice-at-universities-runs-far-deeper-than-racist-memorials/412207/.

---. *Lower Ed: The Troubling Rise of For-Profit Colleges in the New Economy*. New Press, 2018.

Daut, Marlene L. "Becoming Full Professor While Black." *Chronicle of Higher Education*, July 28, 2019, https://www.chronicle.com/article/Becoming-Full-Professor-While/246743.

Delbanco, Andrew. *College: What It Was, Is, and Should Be*. Princeton, 2012.

Desilver, Drew. "A majority of U.S. colleges admit most students who apply." *Pew Research Center*, April 9, 2019, https://www.pewresearch.org/fact-tank/2019/04/09/a-majority-of-u-s-colleges-admit-most-students-who-apply/.

Dhingra, Pawan. *Hyper Education: Why Good Schools, Good Grades, and Good Behavior Are Not Enough*. New York University Press, 2020.

Dixon-Roman, Ezekiel, et al. "Race, Poverty and SAT Scores: Modeling the Influences of Family Income on Black and White High School Students' SAT Performance." *Teachers College Record*, vol. 115, April 2013, pp. 1-33.

Dweck, Carol S. *Mindset: The New Psychology of Success.* Ballantine Books, 2007.

"Economic Diversity and Student Outcomes at America's Colleges and Universities: Find Your College." *The New York Times*, 2017, https://www.nytimes.com/interactive/projects/college-mobility/.

Editorial Board. "The America We Need." *New York Times*, April 19, 2020, https://www.nytimes.com/2020/04/09/opinion/sunday/coronavirus-inequality-america.html.

Elliott, Larry. "World's 26 Richest People Own as Much as Poorest 50%, says Oxfam." *The Guardian*, January 20, 2019, https://www.theguardian.com/business/2019/jan/21/world-26-richest-people-own-as-much-as-poorest-50-percent-oxfam-report.

Ellis, Lindsay. "For Colleges, Protests Over Racism May Put Everything On the Line." *Chronicle of Higher Education,* June 12, 2020, https://www.chronicle.com/article/For-Colleges-Protests-Over/248979?cid=wsinglestory_hp_1a.

Enyon, Bret, and Laura M. Gambino. *High-Impact ePortfolio Practice: A Catalyst for Student, Faculty, and Institutional Learning.* Stylus Publishing, 2017.

Espinosa, Lorelle L., et al. "Rankings, Institutional Behavior, and College and University Choice: Framing the National Dialogue on Obama's Ratings Plan." *American Council on Education and Center for Policy Research and Strategy Issue Brief*, March 2014, http://citeseerx.ist.psu.edu/viewdoc/download?doi=10.1.1.649.8596&rep=rep1&type=pdf.

Ferrall, Jr., Victor E. *Liberal Arts at the Brink.* Harvard University Press, 2011.

Fingerhut, Hannah. "Republicans skeptical of colleges' impact on U.S., but most see benefits for workforce preparation." *Pew Research Center*, July 20, 2017, https://www.pewresearch.org/fact-tank/2017/07/20/republicans-skeptical-of-colleges-impact-on-u-s-but-most-see-benefits-for-workforce-preparation/.

Fink, L. Dee. *Creating Significant Learning Experiences: An Integrated Approach to Designing College Courses.* Jossey-Bass, 2013.

Friedman, Milton. "A Friedman Doctrine—The Social Responsibility Of Business Is to Increase Its Profits." *New York Times Magazine*, September 13,

1970, https://www.nytimes.com/1970/09/13/archives/a-friedman-doctrine-the-social-responsibility-of-business-is-to.html.

Gannon, Kevin. *Radical Hope: A Teaching Manifesto*. West Virginia University Press, 2020.

Givan, Rebecca Kolins. "Will the University That Survives Have Been Worth Saving?" *The Chronicle of Higher Education*, June 2, 2020, https://www.chronicle.com/article/Will-the-University-That/248902?cid=wsinglestory_hp_1a.

Gladwell, Malcolm. "Food Fight," http://revisionisthistory.com/episodes/05-food-fight.

Gomory, Ralph, and Richard Sylla. "The American Corporation." *Daedalus*, vol. 142, no. 2, Spring 2013, pp. 102-118.

Gregory, Anne, et al. "The Achievement Gap and the Discipline Gap: Two Sides of the Same Coin?" *Educational Researcher*. vol. 39, no. 1, January/February 2010, pp. 59-68.

Hacker, Andrew, and Claudia Dreifus. *Higher Education? How Colleges Are Wasting Our Money and Failing Our Kids—And What We Can Do About It*. St. Martin's, 2011.

Hansen, Sarah. "Grateful Grads 2018—200 Colleges With The Happiest, Most Successful Alumni." *Forbes*, August 21, 2018, https://www.forbes.com/sites/sarahhansen/2018/08/21/grateful-grads-2018-200-colleges-with-the-happiest-most-successful-alumni/#23f091321a0a.

Harlan, Jessica, and Stephanie Marken. "Black College Grads Report Less Support in College." *Gallup*, June 17, 2020, https://news.gallup.com/poll/312548/black-college-grads-report-less-support-college.aspx.

Hartlep, Nicholas D., and Daisy Bell, editors. *Racial Battle Fatigue in Faculty: Perspectives and Lessons from Higher Education*. Routledge, 2020.

Harris, Adam. "When Disadvantaged Students Overlook Elite Colleges." *The Atlantic*, April 16, 2018, https://www.theatlantic.com/education/archive/2018/04/when-disadvantaged-students-overlook-elite-colleges/558371/.

---. "The Little College Where Tuition Is Free and Every Student Is Given a Job." *The Atlantic*, October 11, 2018, https://www.theatlantic.com/education/archive/2018/10/how-berea-college-makes-tuition-free-with-its-endowment/572644/.

Harvard Business Review Staff. "How Companies Can Profit from a 'Growth Mindset.'" *Harvard Business Review*, November 2014, https://hbr.org/2014/11/how-companies-can-profit-from-a-growth-mindset.

Harvard Graduate School of Education. *Turning the Tide. Inspiring Concern for Others and the Common Good Through College Admissions.* Making Caring Common, https://static1.squarespace.com/static/5b7c56e255b02c683659fe43/t/5bae62a6b208fc9b61a81ca9/1538155181693/report_turningthetide.pdf.

Harvey, David. *A Brief History of Neoliberalism*. Oxford, 2005.

Heilig, Julian Vasquez, et al. "Considering the Ethnoracial and Gender Diversity of Faculty in United States Colleges and University Intellectual Communities." *STCLH Hispanic Journal of Law & Policy*, 2019, pp. 1-31.

Hiltonsmith, Robert. "Pulling Up the Higher-Ed Ladder: Myth and Reality in the Crisis of College Affordability." *Demos*, May 5, 2015, https://www.demos.org/sites/default/files/publications/Robbie%20admin-bloat.pdf.

Holland, Megan M. *Divergent Paths to College: Race, Class and Inequality in High Schools*. Rutgers, 2019.

Hurston, Zora Neale. "How It Feels To Be Colored Me," https://www.casa-arts.org/cms/lib/PA01925203/Centricity/Domain/50/Hurston%20How%20it%20Feels%20to%20Be%20Colored%20Me.pdf.

Jack, Anthony. *The Privileged Poor: How Elite Colleges Are Failing Disadvantaged Students*. Harvard, 2019.

Jacob, Brian, et al. "College as Country Club: Do Colleges Cater to Students' Preferences for Consumption?" *Journal of Labor Economics*, vol. 36, no. 2, April 2018, pp. 309-348.

Jaquette, Ozan, and Karina Salazar. "Colleges Recruit at Richer, Whiter High Schools." *New York Times*, April 13, 2018, https://www.nytimes.com/interactive/2018/04/13/opinion/college-recruitment-rich-white.html.

Jaschik, Scott. "Turmoil at the Mount." *Inside Higher Ed*, Feb. 15, 2016, https://www.insidehighered.com/news/2016/02/15/mount-st-marys-reinstates-professors-it-fired.

---. "'U.S. News' Will Rank Test-Blind College." *Inside Higher Ed*, June 22, 2020, https://www.insidehighered.com/admissions/article/2020/06/22/us-news-will-rank-test-blind-colleges.

Keeling, Richard P., and Richard H. Hersh. *We're Losing Our Minds: Rethinking American Higher Education*. Palgrave Macmillan, 2012.

Keels, Micere. *Campus Counterspaces: Black and Latinx Students' Search for Community at Historically White Universities*. Cornell, 2019.

Kendi, Ibram X. *How to be an Antiracist*. One World, 2019.

Koch, James V. *The Impoverishment of the American College Student*. Brookings, 2019.

Kuh, George D. "Built to Engage: Liberal Arts Colleges and Effective Educational Practice." *Liberal Arts Colleges in American Higher Education*, edited by Francis Oakely, American Council of Learned Societies, 2007, pp. 122-50.

Larkin, Max, and Mayowa Aina. "Legacy Admissions Offer An Advantage—And Not Just At Schools Like Harvard." *NPR Education*, November 4, 2018, https://www.npr.org/2018/11/04/663629750/legacy-admissions-offer-an-advantage-and-not-just-at-schools-like-harvard.

Laymon, Kiese. "My Vassar College Faculty ID Makes Everything OK." *Gawker*, November 29, 2014, https://gawker.com/my-vassar-college-faculty-id-makes-everything-ok-1664133077.

Leonardo, Zeus. *Race, Whiteness and Education*. Routledge, 2009.

Lewis, Lionel S. *Cold War on Campus. A Study of the Politics of Organizational Control*. Transaction, 1989.

Lips, Karin Agness. "Stop Creating Campus Bubbles." *Forbes*, November 30, 2016, https://www.forbes.com/sites/karinagness/2016/11/30/stop-creating-campus-bubbles/#78c2bd86372a.

Lukianoff, Greg, and Jonathan Haidt. *The Coddling of the American Mind: How Good Intentions and Bad Ideas Are Setting Up a Generation for Failure*. Penguin Books, 2019.

Markovits, Daniel. *How America's Foundational Myth Feeds Inequality, Dismantles the Middle Class, and Devours the Elite*. Penguin, 2019.

Martin, Rachel. "For The First Time Since World War II, National Spelling Bee Is Canceled." *NPR Morning Edition*, May 28, 2020, https://www.npr.org/2020/05/28/863605657/for-the-first-time-since-world-war-ii-national-spelling-bee-is-canceled.

Martinez-Saenz, Miguel, and Steven Schoonover Jr. "Resisting the 'Student-as-Consumer' Metaphor." *AAUP*, November-December 2014, https://www.aaup.org/article/resisting-student-consumer-metaphor#.XvpJk_J7k8Z.

Medina, Jennifer, et al. "Actresses, Business Leaders and Other Wealthy Parents Charged in U.S. College Entry Fraud." *New York Times*, March 12, 2019, https://www.nytimes.com/2019/03/12/us/college-admissions-cheating-scandal.html?action=click&module=Top%20Stories&pgtype=Homepage.

Menand, Louis. "The Limits of Academic Freedom." *The Future of Academic Freedom,* edited by Louis Menand. Chicago, 1996, pp. 3-20.

@michaelsorrell. Twitter, 15 April 2020, twitter.com/bvisger/status/1250474041355440128?s=20.

Milkova, Liliana, and Steven S. Volk. "Transfer: Learning in and Through the Academic Museum." *Advancing Engagement: A Handbook for Academic Museums, Vol. III*, edited by Stefanie S. Jandl and Mark S. Gold, Edinburgh, UK, MuseumsEtc, 2015, pp. 28-63.

Miller, Arthur I. *Colliding Worlds: How Cutting Edge Science Is Redefining Contemporary Art*. W. W. Norton, 2014.

Morphew, Christopher, et al. *Changes in Faculty Composition at Independent Colleges*. Council of Independent Colleges, 2016.

National Center for Education Statistics. "Race/Ethnicity of College Faculty," 2019, https://nces.ed.gov/fastfacts/display.asp?id=61.

National Institute on Alcohol Abuse and Alcoholism. "Fall Semester—A Time for Parents To Discuss the Risks of College Drinking," 2019, https://www.niaaa.nih.gov/sites/default/files/publications/NIAAA_BacktoCollege_Fact_sheet.pdf.

Nichols, Andrew Howard, and José Luis Santos. *A Glimpse Inside the Coffers: Endowment Spending at Wealthy Colleges and Universities*. The Education Trust, 2016, https://edtrust.org/wp-content/uploads/2016/08/EndowmentsPaper.pdf.

Nova, Annie, and John W. Schoen. "College applicants from wealthy families have an edge, analysis shows." *CNBC*, March 22, 2019, https://www.cnbc.com/2019/03/22/college-applicants-from-families-in-the-1-percent-have-a-big-edge.html.

Oakley, Francis. "Prologue: The Liberal Arts College: Identity, Variety, Destiny." *Liberal Arts Colleges in American Higher Education*, edited by Francis Oakley, American Council of Learned Societies, 2007, pp. 1-14.

Paris, Django, and H. Samy Alim. *Culturally Sustaining Pedagogies: Teaching and Learning for Justice in a Changing World*. Teachers College Press, 2017.

Pascarella, Ernest T., and Patrick T. Terenzini. *How College Affects Students: A Third Decade of Research*. Vol. 2. Jossey-Bass, 2005.

Percheski, Christine, and Christina Gibson-Davis. "A Penny on the Dollar: Racial Inequalities in Wealth among Households with Children." *Socius*, vol. 6, January 2020, https://journals.sagepub.com/doi/full/10.1177/2378023120916616.

Piketty, Thomas, et al. *New York Times*, April 19, 2020, https://www.nytimes.com/interactive/2020/04/10/opinion/coronavirus-us-economy-inequality.html?searchResultPosition=1.

Pritscher, Conrad P. *Brains Inventing Themselves: Choice and Engaged Learning*. Sense Publishers, 2011.

Rankine, Claudia. "Weather." *New York Times Book Review*, June 21, 2020.

Robinson, Marilynne. *What Are We Doing Here?* Farrar, Straus and Giroux, 2018.

---. "What Kind of Country Do We Want?" *The New York Review of Books*, June 11, 2020, https://www.nybooks.com/articles/2020/06/11/what-kind-of-country-do-we-want/.

Rojstaczer, Stuart. "Grade Inflation at American Colleges and Universities," March 29, 2016, http://www.gradeinflation.com/.

Rothstein, Richard. "Modern Segregation." *Economic Policy Institute*, March 6, 2014, https://www.epi.org/publication/modern-segregation/.

Roy, Arundhati. "The Pandemic Is a Portal." *Financial Times*, April 3, 2020, https://www.ft.com/content/10d8f5e8-74eb-11ea-95fe-fcd274e920ca.

Schanzenbach, Diane Whitmore, et al. "Eight Economic Facts on Higher Education." *The Hamilton Project*, Brookings, April 2017, https://www.brookings.edu/wp-content/uploads/2017/04/thp_20170426_eight_economic_facts_higher_education.pdf.

Schinske, Jeffrey, and Kimberly Tanner. "Teaching More By Grading Less (or Differently)." *CBE—Life Sciences Education*. vol. 13, Summer 2014, pp. 159–166.

Schisler, Rebecca, and Ryan Golden. "Mount President's Attempt to Improve Retention Rate Included Seeking Dismissal of 20-25 First-Year Students." *The Mountain Echo*, January 19, 2016, http://msmecho.com/2016/01/19/mount-presidents-attempt-to-improve-retention-rate-included-seeking-dismissal-of-20-25-first-year-students/.

Schuster, Jack H., and Martin J. Finkelstein. *The American Faculty: The Restructuring of Academic Work and Careers.* Johns Hopkins University Press, 2006.

Selingo, Jeffrey. "How to Normalize the College Search Process for Juniors." *New York Times*, June 3, 2020, https://www.nytimes.com/2020/06/03/well/family/college-search-class-of-2021-coronavirus.html.

Sifford, Elena FitzPatrick, and Ananda Cohen-Aponte. "A Call to Action." *Art Journal*, vol. 78, no. 4, 2019, pp. 118-122.

Simon, Caroline. "Bureaucrats and Buildings: The Case For Why College Is So Expensive." *Forbes*, September 5, 2017, https://www.forbes.com/sites/carolinesimon/2017/09/05/bureaucrats-and-buildings-the-case-for-why-college-is-so-expensive/#4f8c1763456a.

Stiglitz, Joseph E. *The Price of Inequality.* Norton, 2012.

Stripling, Jack. "The Lure of the Lazy River." *Chronicle of Higher Education,* October 15, 2017, https://www.chronicle.com/article/The-Lure-of-the-Lazy-River/241434.

Sunstein, Cass R. "The Siren of Selfishness." *New York Review of Books*, April 9, 2020, https://www.nybooks.com/articles/2020/04/09/ayn-rand-siren-selfishness/.

Svrluga, Susan. "University president allegedly says struggling freshmen are bunnies that should be drowned." *Washington Post*, January 19, 2016, https://www.washingtonpost.com/news/grade-point/wp/2016/01/19/university-president-allegedly-says-struggling-freshmen-are-bunnies-that-should-be-drowned-that-a-glock-should-be-put-to-their-heads/.

Swarns, Rachel L. "Crowded Out of Ivory Tower, Adjuncts See a Life Less Lofty." *New York Times*, January 19, 2014, https://www.nytimes.com/2014/01/20/nyregion/crowded-out-of-ivory-tower-adjuncts-see-a-life-less-lofty.html?_r=0.

Swinton, OH. "The Effect of Effort Grading on Learning." *Economics of Education Review*, vol. 29, 2010, pp. 1176–1182.

Tavernise, Sabrina, and Albert Sun. "Same City, but Very Different Life Spans." *New York Times*, April 28, 2015, https://www.nytimes.com/interactive/2015/04/29/health/life-expectancy-nyc-chi-atl-richmond.html?searchResultPosition=2.

Thorp, H. Holden. "Suspend Tests and Ranking." *Science*, May 22, 2020, https://science.sciencemag.org/content/368/6493/797.

"Tuition Costs of Colleges and Universities." *National Center for Education Statistics*, https://nces.ed.gov/fastfacts/display.asp?id=76.

Turner, Cory, et al. "Why America's Schools Have A Money Problem." NPR-Morning Edition, April 18, 2016, https://www.npr.org/2016/04/18/474256366/why-americas-schools-have-a-money-problem.

Valbrun, Marjorie. "Discount Rate Hits Record Highs." *Inside Higher Ed*, May 10, 2019, https://www.insidehighered.com/news/2019/05/10/nacubo-report-shows-tuition-discounting-trend-continuing-unabated.

Volk, Steven. "Sermon on 'The Mount.'" *After Class: Education and Democracy*, February 22, 2016, https://steven-volk.blog/2016/02/22/sermon-on-the-mount/.

"Which Colleges Have the Largest Endowments?" *Chronicle of Higher Education*, January 31, 2019, https://www.chronicle.com/article/Which-Colleges-Have-the/245587.

Wiles, Russ. "Do I want to work for that CEO?" *USA Today*, July 7, 2019, https://www.usatoday.com/story/money/2019/07/07/new-data-show-wealth-gap-between-ceos-and-workers-and-fuel-debate/1667944001/.

Woodhouse, Kellie. "Widening Wealth Gap." *Inside Higher Ed*, May 21, 2015, https://www.insidehighered.com/news/2015/05/21/rich-universities-get-richer-are-poor-students-being-left-behind.

Zaloom, Caitlin. *Indebted: How Families Make College Work at Any Cost.* Princeton University Press, 2019.

Zemsky, Robert, et al. *The College Stress Test.* John Hopkins, 2020.

Acknowledgements

I've always believed that writing is a collaborative process. Now I understand in my bones what that really means. My deepest thanks to Steve Volk for going on this strange, pandemic-fueled adventure with me, despite only knowing me for two weeks when we started! This has been such a rewarding experience. ... I hope we'll actually meet face to face someday. Thanks to Anne Trubek for her energy and passion and spirit of adventure, to Mike Jauchen for his attentive and thoughtful editing, to Martha Bayne for shepherding us through the final steps, and to the entire Belt team. So delighted to be working with all of you! As always, and especially now, thank you to my husband, Jim, and sons, Cam and Tobey, for being exactly who they are, and inspiring me to be who I am. Let's carpe every diem.
—*Beth Benedix*

While I certainly wouldn't "dedicate" this book to the COVID-19 pandemic, I must acknowledge the role the virus played in its completion. Without a lockdown to keep me chained to my desk for the long months of 2020 and the sense of urgency it fostered, I am quite convinced this project would have remained just one idea among many jotted on slips of paper that litter my desk. And, just as likely, without the forced shift to Zoomlandia, I might never met my collaborator, Beth Benedix. This dreadful pandemic has already generated its fair share of stories featuring bizarre coincidences and unusual outcomes, and this book—generated via countless hours of conversation but not a single in-person meeting—is but a small one. I am profoundly grateful for Beth's insights, energy, determination, and wisdom. Each of our conversations shifted the project's focus in small, but significant ways, so that the book that emerged, with all its strengths and flaws, barely resembles where we began. And thank goodness, and thank you, Beth, for that.

It's hard to know to whom I owe thanks for their good thinking about liberal education over a lifetime spent teaching undergraduates. From my long years in Oberlin's history department, Gary Kornblith, Carol Lasser, Heather Hogan, Len Smith, and Ellen Wurtzel were (and remain) good friends and superlative interlocutors. Oberlin also offered me an abundance of colleagues with whom I could share thoughts, complaints, and hopes. Among the many are Liliana Milkova, Tania Boster, Sebastiaan Faber, Albert Borroni, Barbara Sawhill, Marcelo Vinces, Ray English, and Tom Van Nortwick. Many colleagues welcomed me with open arms when I turned my attention to the teaching and learning community outside of Oberlin, among them Alison Pingree, Alison Cook-Sather, and Peter Felten. The Great Lakes Colleges Association has provided me a community and a platform, and I am deeply grateful to Greg Wegner, Sarah Bunnell, Jocelyn McWhirter, Ted Mason, Aimee Knupsky, Frank Hassebrock, Claudia Thompson, Kiran Cunningham, Warren Rosenberg, Deanne Bell, and Joanne Stewart, among many others. I have had the honor of collaborating with generations of remarkable students, many of whom are now professors and educators in their own right. At the risk of overlooking so many, I must thank Marian Schlotterbeck, Jonathan Ablard, Justin Wolfe, Francisco Dominguez, Ben Rosenthal, Victoria Gonzalez-Rivera, Jackie Downing, Max Friedman, Emma Budwig, Tamara Lea Spira, Claire Kinsley, Sam Byrd, Allegra Fonda-Bonardi, Matt VanFossan, Alice Ollstein, Helen Kramer, and Robin Cornell, for all you have given me. Thanks to Anne Trubek, at Belt Publishing, for encouraging and speeding this project along, and to Mike Jauchen and Martha Bayne for their careful editorial work. Finally, this work wouldn't have been conceivable, let alone completed, without the knowledge and support of my partner for more than a half century, Dinah Volk. Her profound understanding of learning and teaching, gained as a professor of early childhood education and as a practitioner in the field, and her ever-deepening understanding of what it means to be a culturally sustaining teacher and to work towards an anti-racist pedagogy continue to shape my thinking, and to suggest just how much more remains to be learned and put into practice. Needless to say, the errors and shortcomings in the text are on our shoulders; the work yet to be done … that's on all of us! —*Steve Volk*